£3

D1458418

MEMOIRS
OF AN
ART THIEF

MEMOIRS
OF AN
ART THIEF

Edward Moat

Arlington Books
Bury Street St. James's
London

MEMOIRS OF
AN ART THIEF

First published 1976 by
Arlington Books (Publishers) Ltd
38 Bury Street St. James's
London SW1

© 1976 Edward Moat
printed and bound in England by
The Garden City Press Limited
London and Letchworth

ISBN 85140 238 0

Part One

I first got the taste, as they say, beside the Rhine in March 1945. I was sitting in a tent pitched in a small wood behind Xanten. It had been soaked by icy rains that had sluiced down for the three days since we had moved up. As each salvo from Monty's wheel-to-wheel guns roared overhead a shower of miserably-minded drops shook down, to find all the usual places for spreading discomfort. We should have been over by now, but the orchestration of the guns had had to be reduced to sharp chords rather than the rumbling thunder that Monty had made his trademark. The reason, labour troubles back at Tilbury over the loading of the ammunition we needed to wipe the job off.

An army tent, official issue, is not the most comfortable place for a week-end, especially with just a camp-bed and packing-case. When the word came down the lines that the crossing was postponed for up to ten days, the period necessary to restart the supply line moving, I decided to do something about comfort. From where I was pitched I could just see the Rhine in full spate, ice-grey, on its way to the North Sea. The view was vignetted by the trunks of beech trees which were supposed to be hiding us from what remained of the Greater Reich Armies. The result was not completely effective, as every now and then some offensive spirit on the other side would send an 88 whistling across to splinter into the branches or spew up the mud. Comfort was what I was seeking. Behind our lines lay more woods and the odd hill which was invariably crowned with a schloss or like sombre mass of masonry. Taking the jeep, I tracked away from the mess and the noise and set off on the road to Goch and steered towards one of these symbols of the Fatherland I had spotted. The approach was by a side road and led first past what must have been a kind of lodge, if that was what it had been before something large and explosive had arrived on top of it not long ago. The drive curled up the side of the hill, at times barely a car-width wide. After some five minutes of 'expect what comes next' motoring, quite suddenly it became civilized and opened out in front of one of those erections that only the Germans could ever consider building. It gave the impression that the architect had loaded it with turrets, Gothic arches, steeples, weird chimneys, and the rest; and there stood the result, formidably draped in Teutonic shades of sombreness. The jeep squelched to a halt about three yards from the flight of steps that led up to the front door. I got out and stood for about five minutes just listening. But apart from the ticking of the exhaust of the jeep as it cooled, and the insiduous dripping from numerous broken gutters, there was nothing.

Over the door was a grotesquely carved stone arch featuring some of the more macabre imaginings of Dürer; smeared with grey-green lichens, they stared down at me with protruding eyes, with long teeth bared and forked tongues draped out. Above them set in the cold slimy walls were rows of stern metal-framed windows, all firmly closed. Further up, corbelled mock battlements leaned out, interspersed with gargoyles from the same stable as the beasts over the door.

There is little quite so still as an empty building, or at least one I hoped was empty. Climbing the steps, I gave the verdigrised copper handle an experimental turn and rather surprisingly it moved easily without even a squeak and the heavy bolt-studded door swung inwards. A wave of stale dank air gushed out and I could just see what appeared to be a long and lofty hall liberally hung with the inevitable German hunting trophies and assortments of weapons and armour.

Going inside, I took the precaution of wedging the door open with a heavy oak chair, and then began the exploration. All eight of the rooms on the ground floor had been emptied of everything except a few chairs, some vast refectory tables, and, strewn over the floors, broken cardboard cartons, straw, and other packing material. At the end of the hall on the right was the staircase: stone steps with elaborate balustrades on each side of heavy ironwork ornamented with gilt swollen-bellied nymphs and over-ripe fruit; the hand-rails in bronze about six inches wide. Padding up the first flight, I could glimpse the landing above, which looked as if it were furnished and untouched. So it was. Underfoot were two fine silk Kashan rugs with exquisite reds and blues on ivory grounds. Philistine to even think of putting these on a floor. On the walls were tapestries which, on a closer look, turned out to be Gobelin, probably early eighteenth century, as they appeared to be based on animal and bird compositions by Jean Baptiste Oudry. Little doubt they had been brought back by a rejoicing colonel in the last affray – well, they were about to be onward routed by another rejoicing colonel.

The door immediately opposite the top of the stairs to the first floor gave on to what was a sitting-room. The walls of this room were covered with staid unsmiling Teutonic likenesses. The furniture consisted of a sort of exaggerated chaise-longue, occasional tables, a work-basket, and a massive collection of fire-irons in a fender which could have kept out a Panzer Division. Losing interest rapidly in this collection, I moved down the landing to the next room, which appeared to have been the local 'Von's' study. The walls here were laddered with book-shelves crammed with gold-tooled leather-backs of Goethe, Nietzsche, and the rest. A desk stood in front of the window; there were also three hideous hide-covered armchairs and a threadbare Turkish on the floor. Next again along the landing was better, much better. A print-room. Here some more gifted ancestor must have spread out not only his capital, but also his taste. Dürer, Baldung, Cranach, Schongauer, and also lesser and later hands. It was while I was admiring these that I first heard the noise. At the start I may have confused it with dropping water, but now it was more insistent. There was definitely a thrubbing coming from the ceiling above. So I was not alone. The first reaction was to loosen the Mauser in my shoulder-holster. I had some time ago lost faith in the accuracy of the British Army Issue revolver to hit anything smaller than an eight-acre haystack at twenty-five yards and had put my faith in the sophistication of the Mauser with its comforting load of nine rounds.

The bumping stopped and I, together with the perpetrator obviously, held my breath for about two minutes until it was resumed. Under cover of the noise I crept crêpe-soled out of the room along the landing and up the next flight of stairs to the second floor. As I reached the last of the steps, a hoarse bellow in a low, very low soprano reached my ears. What it shouted I did not know, but the realization of the supposed weaker sex sent a charge of male courage through my legs. I tried the first door, the second, the third, and the fourth before I flushed the foe. There, sitting in a representation of a Gothic apse with upholstery, was an old, old German lady. On a side-table to the left of the chair was a silver tray with bottles of Apollinaris and Steinhager, and a tin of dry biscuits. On a table to her right were a bowl of fruit, a plate with an opened tin of Spam, a tablet of white soap, two bars of Mars, a bottle of Pernod, a packet of a well-known American chewing gum, and, quite incongruously, a box of Bryant & May matches.

For about ten seconds we stared at each other. Then she spoke in a near incomprehensible English: "Please who are you?" but without waiting for me to reply went on: "Let me tell you I haf friends, gud friends. Don't touch me."

Actually I had no intention of such an action. The old valkyrie in front of me must have been breathing on close to ninety plus. "Madam," I said. "I see you have good friends on several sides. I am only interested in a little comfort. We have not met before; it is unlikely we shall meet again."

The crone lit up its eyes and glared across the three metres that separated us. "If you touch any of my things, I-I-I-I sssshh – "

"What?" I replied.

"Vy don't we haf a drink? You are an officer. My son was officer."

A claw reached out to the Steinhager and shot a more than ample measure into a glass following it with an inch of Apollinaris. She did the same into a second tumbler.

"Prosit," defying me to ignore tradition. Oh well, a shot, even a double, of their firewater would help. I downed it, clattered the glass back on the table, gave a mocking click of the heels, a charade of a Prussian salute, and then over my shoulder a barked "Auf Wiedersehen".

On the first floor in the print-room I gathered up the set

of Dürer's 'Apocalypse', and also his 'Prodigal Son', 'Adam and Eve', 'The Sea Monster', 'The Dream', and, best of all, 'The Knight, Death and the Devil'; Martin Schongauer's 'Nativity' and 'Foolish Virgin'; Cranach the Elder's 'Adam and Eve'; and a gorgeous 'Groom Bewitched' by Hans Baldung. I pulled down two of the Gobelin tapestries about nine feet high by six feet broad (just right as bed-covers). Laden, I swooped down the stairs and out to the jeep to load up. Back and up to the first floor again to pull up the two Kashan rugs and to pick up a quite charming easy chair, *c.* 1700–50, which I tried first for size. Down again, and then a final nip up to lift an excellent seventeenth-century bracket clock from the mantlepiece in room four and a bronze animalier of a Russian troika and horses, which I couldn't resist. This last, I suspect, had been nicked by the colonel's brother somewhere about 1917 east of the Dnieper. Until the last swirl round I hadn't realized how catching this taste could be. A delicious feeling somewhat akin to a lavish shopping expedition flushed through me, yet even better because there was little likelihood of an account being presented later. Now all was stacked in the back of the jeep and covered with camouflage netting.

Through the still open hall door I could hear wild Wagnerian noises descending the stairs.

"I shall haf the Red Cross look into you. You steal. You are not proper officer."

Not wishing for a further confrontation with this offspring of Brünnhilde, I started the jeep and lost sight of the schloss as I swept round the corner of the drive.

*   *   *

The last months of the war were not conducive to regrets or for arousing great feelings of sympathy for the enemy. On the long trek from Normandy across France and into

Belgium one had seen too much and heard too many truths. Like many another with the armies, the air force and navy I had hidden away in my private heart a personal moment of harsh tragedy. One could become immured to an extent against violence in action but when that violence was wrought far away behind the lines on one's family it was so different; it became a thing of personal involvement in a manner which blasted away hitherto accepted standards of conflict.

My own moment, that lay deep under layers of instinct-toughened consciousness, was sometime after midnight, May 10th 1941. The place, London, a top-floor flat that had come off second best to one of those ton-up mines that drifted down on emerald-green silk parachutes. Of course it was not just the top flat that went, it was the whole house and most of the street as well. But in the top flat were my father and mother and my sister. Three more digits for the score book of Feldmarschall Hugo Sperrle who liked to declaim 'Is there a foe that bombing cannot break?' Looking back from today, he had his answer from London, not only on the night of May 10th, but also for all those other nights that were before and after.

*   *   *

Some people claim they have childhood memories which go back to exceedingly early days. Perhaps I was a delayed-reaction infant, for I cannot, with truth, recall earlier than my fourth birthday.

That day I do remember as one of firsts: the first time I blew out a candle, one of four on my cake; the first time I managed to get down on to the beach unattended – this was by executing a craftily worked out route through the rhododendrons beside our house, and then crawling along behind the greenhouse, and finally making a hole in the wooden fence by pulling out three rotten boards; the first time I had strawberries with mayonnaise, and the last – this came about because of a lack of correct information from the nearest adult; and the first time I went out in a boat with my father.

The boat, in retrospect, was not exactly a wonder of either power or sail, but it could be made to move with oars, and served well as a platform for fishing from. To me, however, it was certainly the most glamorous vessel that ever floated. A kind of wondrous mixture, part great liner, part battleship, and part clipper, all rolled into one; forgetting, of course, that it needed all too frequent bailing and the bottom was nearly always covered with an array of old tarred ropes, bits and pieces of fishing tackle, evil-smelling left-over lumps of bait, old tin cans, bottles and nameless fragments of rags.

We lived on one of those creeks that abound round the Cornish coast. A small river or tiddler stream wriggled its way down from the hills behind our house and joined with the tides that surged in from the south-west. At low water there was a splendid playground of sand, mud and watery spots, and there was the always changing selection of drift material to be gone through. A few small fishing boats either anchored to a trot or drawn up completed the view to seaward. On land, from my room I could look out to the little village, a collection of small cottages that grasped for a footing under the low cliff and just managed to keep their feet dry with the spring high waters. Our house must have been old; the walls were two feet of granite to keep out the winter gales. The windows had small panes of wavy uneven glass which made the view jump up and down if one raised and lowered one's head when looking out. The grey roof had thick uneven slates mellowed down with orange and green lichen and tufts of deep spongy moss.

My room was in a corner upstairs and had two dark rafters which must have provided homes for many strong-willed spiders, for however much I knocked down their webs, they always seemed to be back again in five minutes. Apart from my room my favourite place was the low-ranging study which was shared by my father and mother. What they did there so mysteriously and earnestly I was not quite sure. But for me there was so much to see and feel. On the wall behind my father's desk were broad shelves which held large cloth-bound scrap-books and these I was allowed to look at. The pages of the early ones were already yellow and cracking but the pictures I could see made me turn and turn again to them. Some were in line only, others were early photographs. They showed old paintings of people, of battle scenes, of palaces, of ships riding out storms. My parents could guarantee themselves at least an hour of peace when they handed me down one of these treasure-houses.

Early years float by, often with surprising speed. By the time four more birthdays had come and gone I had acquired a sister and found myself an inhabitant of that peculiarly British institution, a preparatory school. The one my parents had selected for me was in that belt of such places as ring Oxford, and I suppose didn't really differ much from the next. A uniform of cap, tie and colour-topped stockings worn with the traditional grey flannel suit, shorts until I was twelve and for the last year, as a sign of seniority, longs. Memories here are sporadic. Sunday suppers of dripping and bread. Endless Sunday walks through bramble-tripping paths led by the big-busted junior matron. Lined up in the late evening, also on Sunday, outside the dreaded head's study for the cane. Once when I did by some fluke make the football (or did we call it 'footer'?) second eleven, there was a visit to a nearby

Catholic school for a match. Afterwards they gave us a super tea with lots of beef sausages. Art as a subject in prep schools in the twenties was a practically unheard of matter. We might be allowed to dabble with a few small scraps of paper, hard pencils and crayons in 'hobby' time but the head would have probably thought any parent who suggested doing such a subject was making an indecent suggestion.

The work, and work it really was, consisted of struggling with small blue textbooks by some gentlemen who I think were called Hilliard and Botting and who set out to instil in us the language, as I imagined, of the early Roman centurions and emperors. There was, of course, that awful subject algebra which meant that eventually 'X' would equal 'Y', or that was the position I got to. Then there were history and 'geog' and French. All of this led up to us taking the Common Entrance so as to be able to mount the next step in the curious education pattern. The British have the strangest notions on encouraging their young. At each stage you enter trembling and leave large in the head only to start all over again.

At any rate, egged on with parental pleading and a generous helping of terror-threats from the form master, I passed the exam and entered the confines of the public school system. One that is incidentally misnamed, or certainly was then, for there was never anything less public. The one that my parents had set their hearts on presumably for my benefit had its beginnings well back in history with traditions and strange masochistic customs that were all worked out to produce a conforming end-product. It did at least have one advantage. Not being a town school, it was set in spacious grounds of its own. But it was still a great stone pile for which for my first two years just added up to misery, sporadic fright and fairly consistent hunger.

$\cdot$ $\cdot$

Holidays beckoned, precious periods of time at home, which had now been transferred from Cornwall to that London top flat. For some reason father had had an impulse for the town scene; the beloved house had been put on a long let. No boats, no country; but a marvellous access to those things I found I really wanted to find out more about. London pre-war and still today has an unmatchable collection of treasure-houses. First visits to the National Gallery I can still recall. Wandering round alone and untutored, the pictures must have communicated with me in some strange pure manner that had nothing of sophistication in it. The Victoria and Albert Museum attracted me in another way; the objects in those days were set off in rather a dry manner, but here I could see in the third dimension many of those things that filled some of my favourite paintings.

Back at school, after the usual tremulous first two years, I found myself at every chance in the art room. Not with the intention of trying to force a quite ordinary ability to become a great artist, but rather to soak in the whole meaning of art. Read over again this sounds hopelessly pretentious. Perhaps it was, but I can find no other way of putting it. The glories of a cap for rugger had nothing; the head of the house less. So there I was at the lovely exploring age of fifteen, coming up to six feet, with a shag-head of gold, blue eyes that Bessie, one of the cleaning girls, said worried her, and an ambition to find out just about art.

I must admit that matters did become a little complicated at times. The summer holidays that had held my sixteenth birthday I had spent exploring secretly the anatomy of other people as put down by Velázquez with the 'Rokeby Venus' and Boucher with some of his extravagances. More than this, I gave myself neck-ache many times by standing for long periods in front of panels by Hieronymus Bosch and Brueghel. I must be one of a select few who have inbibed their 'sex education' from such sources.

On my return that winter term I somewhat ill-advisedly began discussing such art matters with Bessie, who, in her primitive fashion, got her wires badly crossed. She whisked me up to an attic to witness a quick disrobing. The hot horror of the moment petrified me, so that before I came to I found she had pulled me down beside her on the dusty mattress and was fumbling with the complicated button system of the male clothing. I was as near as I would ever get to being the victim in a case of rape. But, bless the bell . . . I was saved, as I think at the time I wanted to be, by the heavy-throated tolling for evening roll-call.

As to the rest of my memories of that school, not even the art master, it seemed, noticed any particular talent in me. The remainder of the staff ignored me as one of those social misfits who didn't want to help his house or his school. The head, apart from my initial interview, I don't think ever spoke to me, only acknowledging my presence by the one scribbled word 'Satisfactory' on the termly reports. However, during the last two years at the place something else in me did start to tick because I suddenly realized that if possible I wanted to go to a university to study the history of art and an obstacle in the way was what was then known as the School Certificate. For this I was going to need a language and a science subject in those seven papers which I must pass to get an entrance. So, to the scorn of all, I became a swot, and the more I was derided by red-apple-faced louts, and cynics from the common-room, the more the spurs went in. The shock when the pass-lists were out and my name featured well over half-way up must have mentally castrated many of my ill-wishers, not least my housemaster.

The transition from a public school to a university in the

last half of the thirties I can only say was for me a process of focusing. Life began to arrive in large amounts. A student then lived a life of freedom in a totally different way from how that word is applied today. Perhaps then we were the last of the romantics. The whole heady stream of arriving swept one along head up in what was for me sheer joy. Lectures were windows opening. Study, which was now voluntary and unsupervised, was undertaken with the devoutness of an impassioned monk. Here and there were some moments of earthiness, as well as odd hours spent in Elysium. And, I, together with a high proportion of my age group, discovered that hops made a fair substitute when one couldn't afford the grape.

During those days it seemed I was cocooned in the intimate study of the European Painting Schools and particularly that of the early Flemish and German masters. Indeed, I was so engrossed in my studies both inside and outside the university that I did not pay much attention to what was happening to the map of Europe. It wasn't until late in the winter term of '38 when I met at a party a shy middle-aged curator of one of the small galleries in Germany, who had fled the rising storm, that I had that side of my vision somewhat rudely clarified. One remembers now, all too sadly, the prevailing atmosphere. It wasn't quite hysteria, but on one hand there were the hopefuls waving sheets of paper which ensured peace, whilst undertones of dire warning grumbled away unheeded.

But like so many I went back into my personal hideaway, took my finals, and then, having got them completed, became suddenly filled with a rush of patriotism. I recall how I squandered precious pounds from my always thin bank balance to have a taxi take me and all my belongings from the university. I arrived at my parents' about two-thirty in the afternoon, filled one room of the flat with cases of books and my somewhat scruffy clothes, swallowed a cup of coffee, and then announced I was going round to the recruiting office. There I was met with a mixture of politeness, military bull, and the seriousness required when filling out forms. I was asked at the outset which regiment I might prefer if selected for call-up. This was a bit of a stunner, as my knowledge of the make-up of the British Army was confined to having once watched the changing of the guard and having a near week-end-long bender with three Territorial types.

The second lieutenant who was interviewing me was sympathetic and tried a more roundabout approach by asking me what interests I had apart from the subjects I had been reading at the university. The information with which I supplied him included the fact that I had spent one month of one summer vacation assisting with an archaeological dig. This fact he jumped on at once:

"My dear chap, that's wonderful, you must be a Sapper."

The suggestion did not immediately register and for a moment I sat opposite him and gaped rather vacuously.

"Yes, the Royal Engineers will be just the thing. Now I can't tell how long you'll have before they grab you; might be a few months or just a week or so. Wouldn't be surprised if they don't take you for OCTU almost right away." With that he stood up and shook my hand warmly, and then I was wandering down the street vaguely in the direction of the flat and wondering what on earth the word OCTU could mean – I supposed some code word for security reasons.

The workings of great government offices are a mystery; they always remind me of some enormous kind of one-armed bandit. You put something in and metaphorically press some buttons and then the unpredictable happens. In this case the unexpected was that I received a large buff envelope three weeks later which contained my call-up papers and a rail warrant to the training establishment. By the time September was out I had already arrived at OCTU and was on my way to becoming an officer and a gentleman. No sooner had I the one pip up than with thousands of others I set off on that particularly long trip to Berlin which involved going round by Cairo, the Western Desert, Sicily and Italy from where I was brought back to a staging camp just outside Southampton and then sent on to Normandy. The final time I would see my family was to be for a ten-day leave after I had been commissioned and before I sailed for Egypt. My father was at the time working on minor blitz reporting and my mother was attached to the ARP. Sister Peg was a junior typist in a government office.

After they were all three bloodily removed in 1941 like many another, I suppose, I was subject to a sort of metamorphosis. At first it wasn't something that I recognized. But slowly it was born in upon me during rare moments of reflection that I was altering in outlook. I don't think it was exactly hardening or becoming cynical; it seemed to be more nearly related to the Able Seaman's 'I'm all right Jack', or Machiavelli's 'first law for every creature is that of self-preservation'.

War, to many eyes, may be a team matter, but underlying it all each individual has to fall back to a large extent on the law of the jungle, and after five years the feeling takes on the guise of a habit. During the months since the crash and bash out of the beach-heads in Normandy and the roll-up across France and Belgium – admittedly there had been a pause for the bloody hiccup of the Ardennes – a repeating query had been running through my mind. Just what was I going to do when we finally finished this lot? The cosy world of the dilettante, the scholar, I had envisaged had gone for keeps. At various times during the advance I had sat in the jeep or lain in my tent and rumbled alternatives through my mind. Schoolmastering; trying to bring a little aesthetic enlightenment to repetitive hordes? No. I recalled too vividly red-apple-faced beefy ones; and there would always be the common room filled with people who would be loath to accept an outsider. I might try to enter the museum and gallery world. Mmmmm . . . that wasn't for me. The thought of endless consultations, conferences and the lot, at which people talked at length saying little or nothing, or framed opinions so that it was impossible to know what they really meant – No. The ground didn't seem exactly cluttered with attractive opportunities.

I think it must have been the large sign erected by the Canadians which we passed as we crossed the frontier, and which proclaimed in white letters on a scarlet ground:

YOU ARE NOW LEAVING THE CIVILIZED WORLD.

YOU HAVE BEEN WARNED.

THIS IS GERMANY.

And perhaps it was particularly the first line that started a misty twanging in my mind which for days just wouldn't clarify. Indeed, it didn't until I was sitting in my tent, as I have said, at the back of Xanten alongside old mother Rhine.

My father's estate, when it had been cleared up, left me with some odds and sods of investments that would bring in about £1,100 a year plus the £120 rent from the house – this latter was, however, soon to disappear as I had heard from the tenants that they wished to go. Suddenly, in the midst of my ponderings, the mists had cleared, and with one of those so-called rare flashes of inspiration I decided I would enter the art redistribution trade.

Not, of course, as a competitor to Christie's or Sotheby's,

but working along rather different lines, although with in mind approximately the same profit margin or perhaps more. London, Paris, New York, these had been hideouts for household names in the antique trade for years and I could see little reason why this business should not be headed for the greatest boom ever. In Europe, certainly, the Nazis, under the inspiration of Hermann Goering, had, to say the least of it, confused the ownership question, and this was going to take a long time to sort out, which would be a help. Stories apocryphal and true had always buzzed through the undergrowth. Poor little unfortunates with no knowledge who found treasures in their attics or down the garden beside the thunder-box could expect little mercy when they took their pieces for sale. If the poshest of sharp gentlemen could make an easy thousand out of the ignorance of the seller, they were unlikely to hesitate. Museums were of little help, as they would only bumble some erudite advice about probable age or likely provenance, or possible artist, or maybe the school of, or it might be related to.

I could see loopholes, but at the same time what was burgeoning in my mind would necessitate a lot of research from every angle: not only more art history, but techniques, materials used, the whole gamut; and then, the approach from the law angle – how the lads in blue work, what tools they had, how knowledgeable they are on the subject of art. Added to all this, I must obtain a thorough working knowledge of likely security devices which were in use and keep up to date with those that would be coming along in the future. Last of all, safe ways of disposal must be ferreted out.

Yes, I was going to aim at the top echelons of the art theft business. A gentleman 'lifter' of course; my conscience could be adjusted to removing but not to the use of the rough stuff. My logic may have become a little blurred or shaken by all the bombs, shells and bullets that had missed me in the years. But at that moment as I sat back on my newly acquired easy chair with my feet on one of the Kashan rugs with a glass of Bommerlunder in my hand I was trying to equate my proposed line of action with some of the other hands in the antique business. Was what I intended to do really any more dishonest than the action of a dealer who knowingly sold a fake or a reproduction as the real thing, or jigged up some high-falutin' provenance to take a sucker? These fellows had plenty of pranks to turn the odd coin or Rolls-Royce over to their side. After the second Bommerlunder I decided there wasn't much in it. After the third, and no one should ever have more than three Bommerlunders, I made up my mind I would be the twentieth-century Mr Hood, and, what was more, I wouldn't bother with Mr Scarlet, Mr Tuck or that girl Marian, I was going to work alone. Rob the rich, yes; but none of this distribution to the poor. Where I was sitting was in the Reischwald Forest, not Sherwood.

I put down the empty glass and picked up the bundle of framed engravings, and sorted them out on the bed. The Dürers looked good. I didn't have the time or the materials then to check the edition or even really to give them the once over. The fifteen prints making up the complete Apocalypse were there. This was always considered one of Dürer's major works and had originally been published in 1498. I could see, too, they were all in good condition despite the rather damp state of the castle. There were no signs of those irritating little orange-brown spots called 'foxing' that are so often encouraged by high humidity.

I thought for a moment as to the best way to transport this trove around with me and then realized the obvious method for the prints would be to use one of the large flat pockets of my map case, which was a rather fine one I had haggled off an Arab leather worker in Ismailia back in 1942. It measured about twenty by sixteen inches, had substantial reinforced leather backing, three flat pockets closed by zips and was firmly secured with a heavy flap and lock. Moreover, I had plenty of sheets of thin cartridge paper with which I could interleave the prints. It didn't take very long to get them out of the frames and mounts into which, fortunately, they had been only lightly fixed with small strips of gummed paper, and then all twenty-four were safely stowed under the folded maps of France which I would not be using again. The frames and the rest I disposed of in a thick scrabble of bushes behind the tent.

The clock had me beaten for the moment. By its appearance and somewhat heavy design I guessed at South German. It had a pleasant leisured tick and, five minutes later, I found it also had a sonorous strike – in loudness rather out of proportion to its size. I felt, for travel purposes, it would be best if this were silenced, so I moved the little lever across, which effectively stifled it. The clock and the bronze could be wrapped up in a blanket and put in a case.

Further activity in this line was stopped by the sudden and continuous roar of heavy lorries. A disembodied hand appeared and knocked on the tent-pole.

"Come in, Sergeant. What's all that row about?"

The flap was lifted and my sergeant came in. A good one, he had been with me since our party had been formed in the Western Desert in 1941. We had been originally intended as a specialist unit to deal with out-of-the-ordinary explosive devices, such as booby-traps, and explosive thermos flasks, fountain-pens and other things that Jerry liked to litter his retreats with. The total strength of the outfit had grown, but the size of the unit was always difficult to assess, as it was constantly being split up along the length of the front; an officer, NCO and half a dozen other ranks being the usual size of these splinter parties.

Officer strength ebbed and flowed with good or bad luck and the inventiveness of the opposite side. In January 1941 I had got my second pip and found myself volunteering for this hair-curling outfit. Six months after that one of the captains undid something the wrong way and the 'third pip' weighed down the epaulettes of my somewhat scruffy desert shirt. This appeared to be the order of promotion. After the landing in Sicily I found the major's crown was forthcoming, as the previous second-in-command had had a misunderstanding with a booby-trap in a house; this had knocked him senseless, and then when he was being driven to the First Aid Post the jeep had collected a mine on the road. It was a messy way to become a major.

On returning to the UK the CO must have decided that his luck was getting a bit sparse and he put in for a transfer, leaving yours truly as a Temporary Acting Hostilities Only – more fool me – Lieutenant-Colonel.

Our way of life, apart from the gruesome side of our designed activity, was almost pleasant; one of the private armies, which no one ever seemed to trace and if they did, they were never sure what these groups were supposed to be doing. My sergeant wangled the rations with professional ability. The pay came through somehow. Our transport we supplemented from captured dumps and likewise much else of our equipment.

"Excuse me, Sir, but them bastards have let the bricks come through at last. Give 'em a few hours to unload and we can 'old on to our flipping ear-drums."

I peered out of the tent and it was satisfying to see an endless column of twelve-tonners careering on the way to the gun-lines, all loaded, I should think, well past the safety mark with every type and shape of shell the British Army used.

"Do you fancy a tot of this fire-water, Sergeant?" I pointed to the Bommerlunder.

"If you don't mind, Sir, I think I'll stick to a couple pints of the Belgian beer; it may make yer run but you 'av got some pipes left after it."

"What's on the menu tonight?"

"Well, me and the Corporal 'ad a bit of luck, as you might say, whilst you was out. It's roast pork, Sir, with powdered spuds and tinned tomarters; for afters tinned plums and custard to settle it."

Two days later, in the late afternoon, the sporadic salvoes from the guns around us suddenly stopped. For a few minutes there was an almost complete silence; just the breathing of a light breeze through the sprouting branches overhead, the slight song of some lonely bird. Then, as though some unseen conductor had raised and dropped his baton, the Alamein barrage belched into being. The sound was almost beyond noise, out-shouting Wagner and Siegfried at their best. It was impossible to pick out individual weapons from the magnificent drum-roll that sent hundreds of tons of high explosive and steel to crack and blast into towns, villages and country the other side of the Rhine. It went on right through the night; the flashes flickering violently all along the river front with the effect of some gigantic demented Will-o'-the-wisp. Early in the morning of March 23rd, at another stroke of that controlling baton, again silence.

From the distance behind us began another sound. At first a soft drone, that became a deep mumble which almost instantaneously burst into a head-splitting roar as over the tops of the hills behind us, flying breathtakingly low, came the air armada to beat them all. In lines of dozens abreast and in a column that was already disappearing to the east whilst it still poured over the western horizon came Liberators, Stirlings, Lancasters and Dakotas, all with gliders in tow. In the bright clean sunshine of the morning the final doomknell was sounding off. Earlier, immediately the barrage had lifted, the first predatory fingers of the assault had felt their way across the fierce current of the river and now they were being joined in force. Pontoon bridges were inching their way out from the west bank. Within forty-eight hours the crossing as a thing of danger was over. I motored up to the bridge site and through glasses could clearly see the flame-throwing Churchills of the Guards wriggling their way into the outskirts of Rees, their progress punctuated by livid orange tongues of fire that splattered into the buildings and were immediately hidden by thick clouds of black smoke. The curtains for the infamous Reich were dropping fast.

Six days later we loaded up and crossed the Rhine, following up the advance across the northern plains, which was moving at a great rate. The bright spring days of April went past as a series of movements from one shattered township to the next; the whole scene becoming more and more of a hideous fairy-tale. Sheer gargantuan destruction by all on all sides, and through the quake-wrecked land-scape moved the teams of the actors. Pouring to the east khaki, the light of victory in its eyes; the crackle and thump of weapons punctuated here and there by some lively spirits letting go with the odd hunting horns. Straggling to the west hordes of scowl-faced, grey-green tattered prisoners, having surrendered they scarcely knew to whom; and inter-woven with them pitiful groups of their yesterday's slave-workers, putty skin drawn tight on skulls, pushing prams piled high with their – even if theirs was only a rubbish of tins, rags – possessions so valueless for the journey out of the hopeless night of the twentieth-century Gehenna.

As far as our unit was concerned the job was over; but we carried on with the rest. The roads were inadequate for the traffic. Military police struggled to find alternative routes. Army road signs became muddled. On May 1st we found ourselves away from the main stream on a side road weaving through some woods near Nieder-Haverbek. Rounding a long bend, we had the embarrassing and nerve-tingling experience of coming across what appeared to be a large part of a Panzer division, complete with Tiger tanks, the lot, laagered amongst the trees. The ramrod figure of a Prussian Colonel approached, saluted smartly and informed me that they wished to surrender. In the consternation of the moment I could think of nothing else to say but:

"Good. Montgomery coming," pointing to behind us, and then slamming the jeep into gear and, following my little convoy, roaring round the next bend.

We picked up a signed route again at Salzhausen and followed the signs to Lüneburg. Before we got there we met up with more MPs who were trying to sort out order from the chaos. They eventually sent us up to Winsen where a makeshift staging-post was being organized for 'odd bod' units like ours. My sergeant was an expert by this period of the war at comfort and he found us two comparatively watertight houses where we settled in to wait for Army Movements to come round with orders. May 7th, and unbelievable even when we heard the voice crackling out of the radio, 'Unconditional Surrender'.

It wasn't until May 30th that movement instructions came in. On June 1st we were to back-track to Nijmegen and a holding area. During the waiting weeks of May I am not sure at this distance of time quite what we did do. It seems, however, the time passed to a degree in an alcoholic mist which was interrupted by 'swanning' trips around the district, brushes with the black market – cigarettes became far too valuable to smoke, and for a tin of coffee and two tablets of soap you could as good as buy a house.

When the time came for the journey back to Holland, as the weather was good we took three easy days to make it, and finally pitched on a pleasant camp-site near the power station at Nijmegen. A visit the next morning to Movement Control and I found that we still had another four days to wait. We were booked on an LST from Antwerp sailing to Southampton on June 8th.

Various other parts of the old party had drifted into camp including one of my captains, so there was sweet nothing to do as he took over the running of things. If my recently chosen career was to proceed, I might as well indulge in one last routing about in the area before the sanity of life returned. There might be something someone had over-looked. I had transferred my treasures to date to a large lockable office chest, so now leaving my tent under the watchful eye of my sergeant, I topped up the jeep with juice from the nearby petrol point, strapping on a couple of jerrycans as a reserve, and set off plus trailer with bed-roll.

At the last minute I thought that I would take a look at the bright lights of Brussels on the way and have a solo night out. Accordingly I left on the Hertogenbosch road and from there down to Eindhoven turning west to Antwerp via Turnhout and so south through Boom to Brussels.

Obviously I wasn't aware at the time but this last minute decision to change my plans and visit this city was going to provide me with something very valuable for the future.

Arriving in the capital, I checked my jeep and trailer into one of the military parks, and then, with a small hold-all of washing gear and a clean shirt I walked off through the streets to book in for a room for the night. Brussels is and always has been for me personally a city of excitement and one that seems to be going at top speed, even faster than Paris or Cairo. Turning off one of the main boulevardes, I found the kind of quiet place I wanted. Madame was friendly and charming, and gave me a room at the back. It didn't have a private bath, but there was a magnificent white-tiled general bathroom along the corridor. For over half an hour I enjoyed a steaming hot soak that seemed to remove a large quantity of the staleness and the smell of war, which the odd bucket-splash or camp-canvas-bath just couldn't compete with. After I had dressed once more I wandered off to make a start for the evening.

The first bar I went into was almost empty and was pleasantly and not garishly lit. I ordered a large dry vermouth with a slice of lemon, some soda and definitely no ice. I was about half-way through this when from behind me to the right I heard the sound of raised transatlantic voices. I turned to see two GIs, one a corporal and the other a sergeant, shouting at an elderly man and trying to grab something from him. The sergeant was shaking him fiercely by the shoulders and causing him considerable distress. Not normally one to get mixed up in other people's troubles, I nevertheless felt this was a case for butting in. Leaving my drink where it was on the bar, I went over and tapped the sergeant on the shoulder and said:

"Having trouble, soldier?"

Both of them were the worse for 'hooch'. The sergeant turned round belligerently, glared at me through reddened eyes and told me:

"Get stuffed, buddy. This is my war. You keep out of it." Then his sodden senses must have taken in the pip and crown on my shoulders and he endeavoured to come to attention, caught the back of his knees on a chair and flopped down and remained there looking foolish and trying to salute. I turned to the corporal and said:

"What's up, Corporal?"

He replied: "Gee nothing, Sir. I was just going to – to buy this book off this old fella."

I turned again to the sergeant and said: "On your feet, Sergeant, and both of you get out of here, fast."

The two of them, slipping and staggering, walked out of the door, and the last thing I heard was:

"Ffffing Limies."

I turned to the elderly man at the table.

"Are you all right?"

"Oh yes, Monsieur. I am all right; they have not hurt me. I am very grateful to you, Colonel."

He had a lean aesthetic face with almost completely grey hair which he kept brushed back. His nose and cheeks were well-formed with good bone. His eyes, grey to green, had that quality which could draw one to him. His hands, which still clutched the book, were sensitive with long fingers and well-kept nails. His clothes had once been very expensive but now, many, many times cleaned, had a sheen of age yet still retained their dignity.

"You will let me buy you a drink, Monsieur?" he asked.

"I'll join you first, and finish the one I have over there," I replied. I went over to the bar and fetched my glass and sat down at the other side of the table from him. I offered a cigarette but he said: "No, no, I will have a small cigar." Together we lit up.

"How long had those two been worrying you?"

"Ohhh – only a few minutes before you came in. The Yanks they are souvenir mad. They want to go back to their homes with something someone else hasn't got."

"If you don't mind me asking, why were they after the book you have there?"

"I don't really know, Monsieur, because it is only a book of quite ordinary engravings, not very old ones at that. I suppose the leather binding and the gold work on it may have made them think it was something special. It is nothing."

"Do you live far from here?" I asked him.

"Oh, I don't live in Brussels. My home is away to the south. I have come up here to see if I can find any materials for my trade."

"For your trade?"

"Ah – yes – I paint and I do a little restoring. Before the war I was very busy. But now it is almost impossible to carry on. It is so difficult to get the paints, brushes, the materials that are needed. And you, Colonel, you are a soldier all the time?"

"Ohhh – no, I'm just here for the war, and I hope very soon now I shall be back, as we say, as a civvy."

He signalled the waiter over and two more drinks appeared a minute or two later. "You have a job to go back to I expect, Monsieur?"

"No. I, like many others, had just finished my studies."

A seed of thought was growing in my mind. If I was going to do what I had decided I was going to do, I would have to know a lot more about pictures than just who painted what and when. Could it be that my friend in front of me might be of some help?

"Tell me, Monsieur, about your experiences before the war when you were painting and restoring."

"Ah – yes – one can learn so much at art schools, but it is, I found very quickly, the years of experience, actually working, that give one the knowledge, that give one – how can I say – the sight that one can look at a picture on canvas

3—MOAAT • •

or panel and feel what is there, what is underneath, what the artist did."

I ordered another round and then turned to him and said:

"Monsieur, I feel in you a kindred spirit. Perhaps we can dine together."

The little man said: "No – no – you must dine with me, because you have been very kind and perhaps saved me trouble tonight."

I said: "No, Monsieur. Please let me. You know somewhere round here?"

"As you wish. About three minutes walk there is a good little place."

So after finishing our drinks we went off to his little place. The patron did indeed provide a good meal: an hors d'oeuvres which almost by itself was sufficient to satisfy; this was followed by a fine clear soup; and then a biftek which even if it were cheval was excellent, and with it, at the bequest of my guest, was produced a good red to digest it. Across the table I think we both talked non-stop, about painting, about the make-up of artists, their ways and their means, and I knew that that thought-seed had been correct. Here was someone who could be a very great help to me. By the end of the evening he had begged me to call him André and I had responded with "Call me Edward".

I had gently to deceive him just a little, to give him the impression that I was a collector in a small way, a connoisseur, perhaps with the suggestion of the dilettante, and someone who wanted to know more about the matters we had been touching on. As we parted he gave me his address and full name. I told him that unfortunately at the moment I couldn't give him an address as my family had been bombed out in 1941. But I would give him somewhere to write to as soon as I could. In any case, I did hope to return to Belgium in the not-too-distant future. He had given me an invitation to visit him in his home if I were in that direction, which he had hoped I would be. So I now even went so far as to suggest that if there were a small hotel nearby perhaps I could stay there for a few days and we could continue our most interesting discussion. He seemed delighted at the idea. And so we left it, after much back-slapping and squeezing of hands.

I returned to my hotel and after a very sound sleep was called the next morning with a cup of coffee like black dynamite and a croissant. By half past eight I had made my way back to the military car park, picked up my jeep and trailer, and was on my way to start the 'swan'. I headed first of all towards Liège, thence to Aachen, through Düren and down to Euskirchen. From there I made my way into Mechenheim and towards that somewhat strange area of the Eifel, a volcanic plateau which lies between the rivers Rhine, Mosel, Ahr and Our. The bleak uplands rise to some two thousand five hundred feet above sea-level and are pitted with small crater lakes and pimpled with defunct volcanic cones. The district is cut through with sudden valleys and at times shrouded in heavy woodlands.

The jeep purred its way along winding side-roads which became more narrow and more serpentine. Unknown to me, I was coming up on a slice of fate or fortune. Halfway down a particularly steep hill I came across an entrance of a kind. On the right what was little more than a wide footpath made off into the trees. I stopped the jeep and the first thing that caught my eye was that unlike practically every other lane, track or path which bore numerous tyre marks this one showed evidence of only a single set of tyres, and what was more, whoever had driven the car or whatever it was had done so at a fair old speed because the tracks showed slides and skid marks. Whether the driver had been coming out or going in I had no way of knowing. Nudging the Mauser under my left arm with my elbow, I decided to have a look. Within twenty yards from the road the path had turned so violently and entered trees so thick that it would have been invisible to passing traffic. After about three-quarters of a mile the woods thinned slightly to let some daylight through from overhead, and then round just one more twist I came to a small clearing, in the middle of which sat a house. Cautiously I drove right round it, but there was no trace of any other vehicle. Whoever it was who had been in a hurry, they had been going out. I finally parked the jeep on the far side of the house, so it was hidden from the entrance path and then I got out, lit a cigarette and strolled round the building, glancing in at the windows. Not a moving thing to be seen; the only sounds the relentless dripping from the trees and the faint dribble of running water from below.

Picking up a torch from the jeep and taking the Mauser in my hand, I went up to what appeared to be the back door and gave it a cautious boot with my foot. Groaning slightly and scuffing the stepstone, it swung inwards. Imitating all the best points from commando lessons on entering suspicious buildings, I gave that house a thorough run-through. There was nothing; that is, nothing living, or dead for that matter. But there were plenty of signs of a very hurried skip indeed. In the kitchen a half empty bottle of Asbach was on the table with its cork beside it. On a plate were the stale remains of a savoury sausage. Over the back of a chair had been flung an SS greatcoat. Lying on their sides under the table were a pair of jackboots. On the window sill lay a small pile of letters. I picked up the top two or three envelopes and noted that they were addressed to a middle of the road ranking type called Ernst Braun.

The strangest thing of all was that in the weeks I had

been in Germany I had not come across a house before that had not been shaken up by some other looting bastard either from our troops, the Yanks or the local talent. Here was virgin territory – if that term were applicable. I had time and would skin it if necessary to make sure Herr Braun had not left anything worthwhile. The signs all seemed to say that he had been caught with his lederhosen down by the speed of the Allied advance and had taken off like a rocket and, what was more, probably in civvy clothes. Good luck to him and Good luck to me.

The kitchen fine-art-wise was a blank, although I did fill up a large carton of goodies from his larder: jars of fruit in brandy, tins of foie gras, tins of those likeable Nuremberg herb sausages, sundry bottles of local wines and while I was at it I cleared his entire stock of some twenty bottles of French liqueurs. The kitchen could be reached apart from the back door by an entrance from the hall. This latter place was large and all but barren: just three heavy oak chairs, a massive stone fireplace, and overhead rows of hunting trophies. The other door across the hall opened into what was the living- and dining-room combined. Again the beloved cumbersome, comfortless heavy furniture. On the floor a rather second-rate but expensive carpet. There were also dark brown voluminous velvet curtains and some light fittings of gross glass with thick metal frames. The walls gave better promise. Between the windows opposite the door appeared to be an early 'Madonna', close around the time of the early Flemish painter Robert Campin. The adding machine that is closely linked with my eye started to go off like a November 5th Catherine Wheel. I walked towards the picture quickly and lifted what I hoped was a precious trophy from the wall. It looked good. The paint surface seemed right, and it was obviously painted on wood. I turned it over and there in painstaking Gothic lettering was the label of a firm of Old Master Copyists in Munich. Blast! I threw it down and went along to the next picture, which was one of those torture-cum-corpse compositions beloved by Pieter 'Hell' Breughel. This time I examined the back first; the result was the same as the previous one. This also applied to a seeming Memling of an 'Adoration', as well as a 'Madonna' by Hans Holbein the Elder. The ornaments were in the same class only the reproductions were not as good.

The stairs gave on to a wide landing that lay between the two bedrooms. On this landing the sole furnishings were a black oak table, a thick earthenware bowl of very dead flowers, and a shoddy imitation Beauvais tapestry on one wall. The first bedroom I went into must have been Ernst's because on the floor were his black SS breeches and across the end of the bed the uniform jacket. But there seemed a subtle difference here. Although there appeared to be little to see, what was there had quality. On a small table opposite the bed was a good example of a Reichsadlerhumpen, a beaker of German glass, which I thought might date from about the beginning of the seventeenth century, and which was enamelled with the arms of the Electors of the Holy Roman Empire. Hanging on the wall behind it was an excellent example of an Icon depicting St. Nicholas, which I judged at the time to be Russian, and which subsequently turned out to date from the middle of the twelfth century, having come from Novgorod. It seemed that friend Ernst must have been on the Eastern Front in the early days, whipping the lads into action and having a quiet go through things on his own account. Matters were looking better. I found that my host had conveniently left an empty and roomy suitcase at the bottom of the wardrobe. I pulled it out and lay it on the bed for my packing. On the top shelf of the wardrobe I noticed one of those rather old-fashioned leather hat-boxes. Perhaps father Ernst had been a Uhlan in the first war or something. I yanked it down and was surprised by the weight. Intrigued that it was locked, I took out my jack-knife and unfolded the heavy spike and broke open the old brass lock, to be even more surprised. The hat-box was empty, yet it had been locked. I felt the weight again and, thick leather as it was, something was odd. Ernst was a slyer character than I had given him credit for. The box obviously had a fairly deep false bottom. A little gentle probing with the spike and this lifted up to disclose something wrapped up in a piece of green baize. Putting the package on the bed, I unrolled it to be met with the sight of what looked like an old ewer with somewhat blunted and bruised decoration and also what appeared to be some kind of inscription in Runic characters which at that moment were beyond my knowledge. Although the metal had a dulling rime over the surface, by its colour and weight it was almost certainly gold. I looked into the hat-box again, and underneath where this ewer had been was another bundle swathed in baize. This turned out to be a fine golden dish about twelve inches in diameter and similarly marked to the ewer.

At the time I had no idea what I had run into, other than it must surely spell a fair old sum of someone's crackly. Actually when I put in some research later on, before I sold the pieces, I found that they were just a bit special. Almost certainly they belonged to what has come to be known as the Treasure of Petrossa, a hoard of material that was found accidentally near a village on the eastern slopes of the Transylvanian Alps in Rumania. More than a dozen pieces survive; some are encrusted with semi-precious stones. There are fibulæ and other objects of personal adornment; dishes and ewers; and also some superb open-work baskets in gold. The discovery was made by some peasants who thought the metal was only copper. A wily Greek workman was shown the collection and he saw that the objects were probably gold and bought the lot for a very small sum. Apparently to facilitate packing for transport, the wretch smashed up a number of large pieces; handfuls of garnets and turquoises and other stones of a similar nature fell on the ground. Some of these were picked up by children playing in the area and they were then seen by someone in authority in the district. After a search was made not only more of the stones came to light, but also many of the broken gold objects were found. Sufficient restoration was carried out for the remains of the horde to be exhibited. But their tale of woe was still incomplete; for they were twice stolen from the place in which they were being shown and again mutilated. Miraculously, once more, some were recovered and were again restored. Even what remains of the treasure points to the great quality the rest must have had. It is thought probably that the craftsman or men who produced the Petrossa treasure must have been working in the third or the fourth century AD, and there could possibly be a connection with the Visigoths.

These two pieces alone made the trip to Ernst's place worthwhile. I rewrapped them and placed them in the suitcase together with the Icon and the glass beaker which I had packed in a pillow-case. Apart from suits and coats, the wardrobe was now bare of possibilities. I turned my attention to a vast chest of drawers that was liberally encrusted with heavily carved flowers and miniature Rhine maidens. The bottom drawer was a welter of socks and stockings; the next up rather incongruously held a number of embroidered waistcoats; and the one above numerous shirts and Ernst's underwear – pastel shades in silk, which he could certainly keep, if he came back. It had already struck me that this must be his intention, when matters had cooled down. I didn't think that he would have seriously cleared right off and left the gold plate behind, as it was not all that bulky and could have been carried around easily disguised in some way or other.

The right-hand top drawer proved more successful. Underneath a mass of silk handkerchiefs was a small oval leather-covered box. Inside was a very nice line in pendants, having a large sapphire surrounded by good-sized diamonds. The inner white satin lid bore the name of one of those very pricey Parisian jewellers in gold script. He must have been caught very hot-foot to have left this, and he would certainly be crawling back down his tracks at the soonest possible moment. The case fitted comfortably into one of the breast-pockets of my battle-dress blouse. The left-hand drawer was jammed to the top with a frightful selection of ties, dozens of them. Having routed these out, I found a flat brown paper parcel loosely knotted with some white tape. Inside this was another for the book about Ernst's character; there was a hefty wad of fine lace – I could only think at this stage it must be Bruges. He seemed to have the knack of collecting souvenirs from places his lot had temporarily taken over. Nothing more in the chest of drawers. No other seemingly likely places our friend could have put anything.

The time was now getting on into the afternoon, round about four-thirty. There was the other bedroom that needed attention. I was just about to gather up the case and its contents, when I noticed that the wan light of the lowering sun was lighting up the wall behind the bed and very faintly I could make out the mark of where a picture had hung; the wall-paper was just that little less faded. If Ernst had been in such a rush as to leave the pendant and the gold plate, it would seem unlikely that he would have hurtled off with a large picture. Something murmured it must be there somewhere. I took another look at the wardrobe first, feeling and knocking for false panels or doors – nothing. Moving the case from the bed, I heaved the mattress off and slashed into the spring-covering with the knife – nothing. But what was the boarding under the springs? I jerked the bed up on to its side and found that there was a shallow packing-case which matched up, it seemed, to the mark on the wall. The case was held in place by four turn-buttons. The prospect of treasure-trove did then and still does today produce a heady feeling in me rather similar to a deep inhalation from a fine liqueur brandy. I unfastened the case, put the bed down flat again, and put my find in such a position that it was possible for me to unscrew the side which had been helpfully marked (in German) as the top. There were eight brass screws and as the screwdriver on my knife was not very efficient, it was nearly ten minutes before the last one was out. I lifted the lid and saw that whatever was inside had been carefully wrapped up in soft cloth and tied round with ribbon. Having undone the bows and pulled the cloth aside, I was confronted with an exquisitely painted wooden panel. In the foreground a figure in blue was mounted on a white horse and behind him were other mounted men, with in the background a cliff, some trees, and the tops of some buildings reaching up into a fine fresh sky with fleecy white clouds. The panel was in a simple channel frame, to which had been attached a label that gave rather breath-taking information as to just what the picture was. It was also to set me the first trial of conscience with my career, self-chosen, of art redistribution. The panel was 'The Upright Judges', variously called 'The Just Sovereigns' and 'The Righteous Judges', and it was by the Van Eyck brothers, Hubert and Jan. It had been originally part of the wonderful altar-piece by them which had hung in the cathedral of

St Bavo's in Ghent. The polyptych had always been one of my favourites when I had been studying the Flemish painters. This work, however, had probably had a more lively history than most. It was apparently originally ordered by Judocus Vijd and is thought to have been commenced by Hubert van Eyck and finished by his brother Jan in 1432. (An inscription to this effect was actually discovered in 1823 underneath some layers of old paint on the outer frame which was being removed by the staff of the Berlin Museum.) It is presumed that the polyptych was first hung in the chapel of Judocus Vijd. Documents of 1458 record how a form of masque based on the Van Eyck work was performed in the square at Ghent to celebrate the entry of Philip of Burgundy. Admirers came from far and wide, including Dürer. In the middle of the sixteenth century there are accounts of the taking of moneys from persons who had come to visit the work; also in 1568 Marcus van Vaernewijck noted that the panels had been disastrously cleaned and that what appeared to have been a predella of either purgatory or hell had been destroyed. There are accounts to back up this mutilation, as about this time Lanceloot Blondeel of Bruges and Jan van Scorel of Utrecht were called in to restore the polyptych.

From early days light-fingered gentlemen from all walks of life have had their eyes open for a chance to nick this prize. The first of these was Philip II of Spain; he was under the illusion that as he was spending 50,000 crowns of his father's money to complete the cathedral of St Bavo's he was entitled to have the paintings. He was thwarted, however, because astute members of the chapter persuaded him that Michael Coxie, who was his court painter, could produce a replica which would be at least as good if not better than the original. In 1566 the religious troubles broke out and the work was transferred for safety to the tower. A little later it was stolen by the Calvinists, who wanted to give it to Elizabeth I (of England) as an inducement towards her future help. This plan was defeated by the intercession of a Flemish nobleman, and by 1586 the polyptych was again back in its chapel. It then had a couple of centuries of uninterrupted peace until the Emperor Joseph II of Austria visited St Bavo's and was shocked by the nudity of Adam and Eve, upon which these two panels were removed and stored away in an attic.

The looting commissars of Napoleon lifted the four main central panels and took them away to Paris, where they were put on display in the Grande Galerie of the Napoleon-Museum alongside many other precious masterpieces raped from their rightful places. After Waterloo it was General Blücher himself who supervised the return of the panels from the Louvre to Ghent.

The saga of the work of the Van Eycks hots up in the nineteenth century. In 1816 the Vicar-General Le Surre, when the bishop Monsignor de Broglie was away, sold the folding doors of the polyptych, minus the Adam and Eve panels, to an antique dealer from Brussels. This gentleman onward routed them (through channels best known and understood by the fraternity) to William III of Prussia. (It was William III's collection that was to become known as the 'Kaiser Wilhelm Museum' in Berlin.) While the door panels were in Berlin, admittedly the inscription quoted earlier was discovered, but also they were subjected to a form of surgery. In 1895 the side panels were all sawn in two so that both sides could be displayed at the same time.

Meanwhile, back in Ghent in 1822, the centre panels only just escaped destruction when there was a savage fire in part of the cathedral. As it was, when the main panel was being removed to safety, it was broken in two.

In the first war the invading Germans thought they could

have the rest of the panels to take to Berlin, but all they were to find were the copies by Michael Coxie. Monsignor Van den Gheyn had forestalled them in time by a hasty removal. After the war, sections of the Treaty of Versailles dealt with loot, and the Germans had to give up the panels held in Berlin. By 1923 the great work was once again complete plus the offending Adam and Eve. A few more years peace and then, on the night April 10th/11th 1934, the panel known as 'The Upright Judges' and the now-separated panel of 'St John the Baptist' vanished. The latter was eventually returned, after payment of a large ransom. But the one of the Judges, at which I was now looking, had remained missing. In its place was eventually to be put a copy painted by J. Vanderveken, who worked on the task for some six months using black and white photographs and an earlier copy by Michael Coxie that he had done in 1599 for Philip II. In the early days of 'my war', in May 1940, I was subsequently to discover the Mystic Lamb had been taken for safe-keeping to the castle of Henry IV at Pau. From there it had been grabbed by the Germans in 1942 and had not surfaced again until about a month previous to my 'find', when the Yanks had found it in the Alt-Aussee salt-mines near Salzburg in Austria. It was returned to St Bavo's in October of that year, and, as it happened, I together with my appendages by that time was nowhere in the district.

If one thinks about this little history, it is obvious that I was in good company – a king, priests, an emperor and sundry very high ranking officers, and the rest.

Gently I pulled the cloth-wraps back across the picture and retied the ribbons. Then replaced the lid and screwed it down. Stunned for a moment by my discovery, I suddenly came to and realized that the evening was approaching and I wasn't going to have time to get back to Nijmegen in the light. Understandably, too, the occupation forces were a little trigger-happy about lone figures careering through the night. I found I was faced with really no choice. Whether I liked it or not, I was going to have to spend the night in Ernst's place. Thank goodness it was the beginning of June so that I would only have to put up with about five or six hours' real darkness.

I went down to the jeep and took out the rotor arm and undid some other bits and pieces which would make it nearly impossible to drive away. I lifted out my bedroll and took it into the kitchen. Then I went back to get the Schmeisser machine pistol that always rested between the seats, a few spare clips for it, and a satchel in which were a couple of grenades and one or two phosphorous bombs – these can be great for discouraging unwanted strangers. Back inside the kitchen, I dumped the artillery and went round the windows and doors. There was no doubt, Ernst was a perfectionist. The doors had massive mortice locks, still with the keys, and metal bolts at the top and bottom as thick as my thumb. The windows on the ground-floor and the floor above were all fitted with thick oak shutters which could be latched in place and then secured right across with a solid steel bar. With all this lot barred, locked and bolted, I didn't know why Ernst had run for it. Anyway, after I had tapped a bottle of his best schnapps and sampled a tin of sausages, which brightened up my British Compot rations considerably, my nerves seemed to be settling down well for my vigil.

About two and a half hours of light remained so I tackled the other bedroom. Surprise, surprise, the chest of drawers was stuffed full of a ransom in French silk underwear, ladies for the use of, and the wardrobe was well hung with dresses of all shapes and sizes. I say sizes, because no one lady could possibly have worn all the confections that were on display. My absentee landlord must have a taste for orgies or some such pastimes with the frauleins, etcetera, I thought. At the bottom of the wardrobe there was one medium-sized flat leather suitcase. I hunked this out and swung it on to the bed. Locked like the hatbox. Lock broken with spike on knife. Lid lifted. There was one thing about Ernst, he was not predictable. This time there was an assortment. I believe that in other days and places Ernst and I might have struck up some kind of working agreement. He had the acquisitive spirit. I now turned out on to the bed what looked at a quick glance distinctly like a small jade carving of a buffalo, two small silver boxes with niello decoration showing scenes that appeared to be Russian, something that I took to be an early astrolabe, five interesting spoons that I judged must be early seventeenth century, and eight of those strange paperweights which send some collectors scribbling cheques all over the place, exquisite in craftsmanship they may be, but just not for me, and finally, wrapped up by itself in brown paper, a small illuminated missal. This last was in fine condition, and I was to discover later was by the hand of one, Attavante, who worked in Florence towards the end of the fifteenth century, and who had been a friend of Gherardo, and an imitator of Bartolommeo della Gatta. Matthias Corvinus, King of Hungary, had engaged his services and amongst other works which he accomplished for the king there remained a missal which had found its way to the Royal Library in Brussels. Attavante was actually a miniature painter of high order, as indeed I had already realized the artist (then unknown to me) must be when turning the pages of the little gem I then held in my hands.

I transferred this lot into Ernst's room, and tearing up sheets and a blanket, wrapped them up and packed all away into the larger case in which I had already put the icon, the beaker and the gold.

The light was now getting very low. I went downstairs to bring up my bedroll, the hardware, and, thoughtfully, a bottle of malt whisky I had discovered at the back of Ernst's larder. I didn't know where he'd got this from, but by rights it should, I felt, at least be mature.

I decided it would be in good taste if I took over the guest-room. Having laid down the load, I went back to attend to the stairs. Going down to the hall, I pulled up the long runner rug and, having weighed down one end with one of those vast chairs, I proceeded to lay the rug up the stairs, keeping it taut between the steps and finally holding it at the top with another weighty chair from the landing; only this time I set the chair so that it was just balanced and would tip with the slightest tug from the rug. Even the most cautious foot in the dark would set off this trap. Last, I barricaded the top of the stairs by pulling over the huge oak table and lashing it into place with the cords from two of Ernst's dressing-gowns.

Having just had about three inches of good malt, I began to feel a bit of a looney — Just who was I expecting to storm my castle? But after a time, as the darkness deepened and the malt wore off, I began to realize that there might be all kinds of people, earthly and otherwise, who could be interested in an assault. Strong-mindedly I kept the bottle at a distance, as I was determined not to get sloshed and put at risk all the goodies I had found. A house occupied just by you in a small clearing in a dark forest in an enemy country at one o'clock in the morning begins to run things itself. At first I was convinced that there was complete silence. Then a whole bevy of noises pressed in on me. The woodwork began to creak, deftly imitating stealthy footsteps. Next the Teutonic plumbing set up a weird gurgling, why I didn't know, as I hadn't touched a tap or the what-have-you for hours. By this time all senses were on red alert. Crack, outside something must be moving as a small branch snapped. What to do? This last course was tricky because my heart was now having a go itself. I crept across to the window which I imagined would look out on to where the sound had come from and very, very gently undid the fastenings of the shutters. Opening them just a crack, I tried to peer out. Useless, it was stygian. Refastened shutters and decided, for purely common-sense reasons, a short malt would not hurt. But it is difficult to judge a short malt in the dark, which was probably actually a good thing.

After what I supposed must have been several hours of bowel-squeezing hearkening I did notice that small threads of dim grey light were beginning to show round the shutters. That was enough. I reached for the malt, swallowed generously, lay back on my bedroll, pulled my tapestries round my slightly chilled form, and I was asleep.

By my watch it was ten-thirty when I opened my eyes and collected my senses and courage. A hasty fill up with sausage and a half bottle of light Mosel. Then I loaded up the trophies, reactivated the jeep and with some relief was away, reaching Nijmegen without incident by five o'clock pretty sharp.

The unit caught the LST at Antwerp on June 8th with no bother, finally breaking away down the Schelde at a little after ten p.m., which brought us sailing across Spithead at about nine the next morning. As I drove off the landing craft on to the hard there was a slight jolt as I was faced by a pleasant-looking customs officer. He asked in the nicest possible way if I had anything to declare. To this I replied well . . . Yes I had . . . a box of French liqueurs. He cast the shortest of glances over the stacked jeep and bulging tarpaulined trailer and waved me through. Mental note: I must take some kind of course in nerve control. All my what's-its were going at the double-double.

I had made arrangements for the second in command to take the outfit to the holding camp and said that I would join him there in a couple of days to begin the breaking up routines and all the other business that would eventually land most of us with an issue suit, shirt, tie, socks, shoes, and so on. Having seen them on their way out of the dock area, I aimed the nose of the jeep to the west and by shortly after three I was picking up the keys from the agent who had looked after the property since the family had gone to London before the war. Five minutes chat and I was heading down towards the old house. Only one thing had been overlooked; I had forgotten the tenants had had the house unfurnished so that that was the way they had left it. Yet once again, out faithful bedroll, tapestries, Kashans and all. Out Germanic rations and a splendid picnic. After the unloading of the spoils from the German Main a blissful sleep.

Part Two

When I awoke it was with a slight chilling trauma. I glanced round at the Germanic remains of last night's picnic and at once thought that I must still be in Ernst's place. It took several minutes before I filtered the facts and got up to take in the old-time familiar view from the window. The garden had been altered horribly by the tenants; the old wooden fence had been replaced by some sterile palings painted in sickening blue. But what did it matter, the house was going to be sold?

On the drive, the afternoon before, I had decided that to live in such a place was far too obvious and apart from that it just would not be suitable. I knew that this business about Mr Hood and the art-redistribution trade I had thought up beside the Rhine in March was really for me. What was more, the mental jig-saw that is so often behind outlandish ideas was rapidly falling into a whole. I knew that to succeed I was going to have to go back to 'school' again; not in the accepted sense, but on a much wider basis. I had my degree and it was from there I must make a start. I had got to *really* learn about painting, drawings, prints, and the rest; not just the background of the artists but all about the techniques they used, the pigments, the materials, the whole bag of tricks, so as to have a sporting chance of recognizing the wiles of the fakers, and the dodges of dicey restorers. This I would call period one of the preparation. When that was in good fettle would come period two, which would be as thorough a recce as possible of the defences I would have to penetrate to realize the object of the exercise, and with this would be what I mentally termed period two B, the digging out of sources of information as to where the best prospecting would lie, and the feeling out for what might be termed 'after theft service' or getting rid of the boodle successfully.

At this moment I wasn't quite sure how long all this was going to take; but I was certain that for ultimate success none of the steps must be skipped. It was going to take a few years, yet I had a strange feeling about all this. It might be compared to the kind of ambition that drives someone up Everest or urges a craftsman towards perfection. This was not going to be a slip, run, miss, perspire with fright operation; it was going to be as perfect as I could make it.

With a glass of wine beside me and pencil and paper I roughed out a few figures to show what material support might be available. As I have said earlier, my father's estate seemed to have been reasonably invested and would bring me in around £1,100 a year. There was a nice little nest-egg of the yearly interest from this in the bank which had accrued since 1941, and which I hadn't touched. The house should make, I estimated, about three thousand. I would, I presumed, get some kind of gratuity. Then there was the stuff that I had just 'liberated'. Here, at the moment, I was rather in the dark as to value, and it would be worth while putting in some research before I walked forth with the market-basket down 'do-the-lads lane'. I tried not to let my internal adding machine run away with itself on these calculations. Anyway, all in all there should be enough for creature comforts from this lot for the apprenticeship period. The obvious residence was some little cosy flat in the triangle of Kensington, Earls Court and Chelsea.

After lunch I reloaded the jeep and trailer and drove back to the agent to give him the keys and to instruct him to put the house on the market, and I also gave him the address of my bank for correspondence.

So, back to the holding camp for my demilitarization. This resolved itself into heel-stamping weeks of waiting, doing little else than supervising the proverbial whitewashing of steps and posts and trying to organize interest activities for a lot of types who had but two ambitions in mind, and these were to avoid a Far Eastern draft and to get back into civvy street with the least possible delay. During this period I managed to get myself a mobile store for swag; this was a just-pre-war Humber Snipe Estate. The stately vehicle was built like a civilized armoured car and it made a fine security dump.

I managed several trips up to London by train, to husband the old petrol coupons, and eventually I found a flat. In ways that suited me, it was unique, being over a joiner's workshop in a not popular mews within my selected triangle. It had one entry by an outside iron fire-escape ladder and another from the other side, through a narrow private door and up some conventional stairs. This second entrance came off an almost deserted side-road that filtered round behind a warehouse and a bomb-site.

Further, during this time of *ennui* I had put in many useful hours in the local library and followed up some sources in town and had managed to arrive at a fair idea of the values of my purloined collection. I had drawn on my nest-egg to buy a few sticks with which to furnish the flat and had found a tailor to suit my taste. It was September before the long-awaited release came and I almost physically peeled off my military guise and laid it on the heap of battered lorries, jeeps, rifles, mortars and the rest of the paraphernalia of war that grew daily as some scarecrow memorial to six years of what?

There had been one last binge in the mess, a last round of those schoolboy pranks, climbing round the room without touching the floor, steeplechasing across the battered, bursting old settees, titanic drinking attempts that ended for most outside with excessive and wasteful regurgitation. Somewhere in the early hours those who could still stand joined arms and hands in an undulating circle and swore eternal allegiance with the Scots memorial chant to 'Should Auld Acquaintance be Forgot'.

After one last cup of army brew and a cardboard slice of toast, I wished those who were braving breakfast farewell, and in a few short moments was out of the camp, out of the army, a civilian and even dressed as one, thanks to the acceleration of my order by the friendly tailor.

The temptation to go on a private spree of celebration was very strong but it was just resistible, and that evening I sat down to a quiet glass of beer and a plate of my Nuremberg sausages and worked out an approach to my selling of the German collection.

From my findings, I had reached the conclusion that, except for the Van Eyck and the gold objects, I could get somewhere between ten and fourteen thousand pounds if I put them into an open auction, but this was a course I did not feel I could take for obvious reasons. I had decided anyway it would not be a good idea to sell the Van Eyck or the gold in England as it would be straining even the most eager-beaver dealer's credulity if I were to walk into his shop with these, and it might even lay my project open to risk of disclosure.

I didn't hurry the selling of the other items. I took it quietly, and I was quite amazed at the ease with which the whole operation went off. London, in that latter part of 1945, was a city emerging from a long night and was in a state of light-headed euphoria. Dealer after dealer that I went to seemed reasonable, asked no awkward questions. I realized they were probably diddling me stupid, particularly the character who gave me only three hundred and twenty pounds for the Baccarat paper-weights. But, to a degree, beggars cannot be selectors, and I was learning.

When I had sold the last, which was the package of lace, I found that I had paid into the bank £7,851, £5,000 of which I had invested to tot up my annual income.

I had made various tentative feelers during the visits with regard to the possibility of interest in an early Flemish wooden panel-painting, but sensed that either they did not want to know or they would very quickly become too suspicious if I went any further. I must admit I was getting slightly worried about the disposal of what was obviously a very hot property. Then, strangely enough, as things sometimes happen, whilst I was waiting to bargain over the price for the lace, I heard two men talking behind an ornamental Chinese screen. I don't know whether they were a dealer and a customer or two dealers. But they were discussing in low voices about the disposal of Flemish and Early German panel-paintings and one of them mentioned a dealer and gave his address, nice and clearly so that I was able to note it down. It was in the Alsace area. The voice went on to say that this man would buy almost anything and he was not fussy and would not split, although he was very sharp on the price he would pay.

Something led me to hold on to the panel and the gold. There was no hurry. Already one could sense that the art market was very slowly beginning to awake. Both these properties could only do one thing, which was to appreciate.

Christmas that year I spent alone in the flat. I had exchanged the old Humber Snipe for something not quite so petrol-thirsty, and the under-the-counter coupons plus my whack would make for a reasonable amount of motoring. I picked out a Hillman Minx, which was roomy enough for my purpose at the moment and was much easier to park.

Early in January I had a welcome letter from the agent in the West Country who told me he had at last managed to sell the house for me and had realized £3,300. This sum I again invested, which with other proceeds pushed up my income to make life more bearable during the probationary period that I envisaged might be quite long.

I devoted practically all of the early part of 1946 to delving into the rather darker side of the history of art which had hardly even been hinted at during my former studies. I found that the general looting of the arts was a somewhat deeper subject than mere personal gain. Going back as far in history as the hey-day of the Greeks and the Romans, and to trace elements earlier still, I found there appeared to be almost a form of colonial acquisition in the matter of stealing; buying or selling under pressure, or plain looting, as part of the theme of conquest. For nearly two thousand years many great collections have been built up and then, as there was a shift of power, have been broken up either violently or subtly. There is the example of Charles I of England, who in his time had one of the greatest private royal collections, part of it being the fine Mantuan collection. With the arrival of the Puritans, in time Charles was executed and the paintings were dispersed throughout Europe.

Perhaps, today, it has been proved that overlords with large armies and plenty of bang-power cannot expect to get away with rolling over people, although unfortunately, there are still some die-slow morons at it. Studying round this point then, I realized the process was being slowly up-dated. There was an almost imperceptible attitude emerging. There was growing gradually a form of more insidious purloining of a people's or a civilization's creative treasures.

As the years have passed since the war, it has become increasingly obvious, too, that a fairly large percentage of those buying works of art are doing so in a manner similar to buying a property or stocks and shares which they feel must appreciate. It seems to me, in retrospect, that I felt the approach of this new climate in collecting. I just wanted a little time and I might be able to satisfy some of their requirements.

Researching into the storehouses of treasures, whether these were national or provincial galleries and museums, private houses, or churches, soon it appeared to me that on the whole the luck was really heavily with the thief. There must be millions, perhaps better to say hundreds of thousands, of interesting objects of value, rarity and beauty to choose from, and to have all these guarded individually round the clock would not be feasible. There must be many large loop-holes if one patiently searched them out. So ran my thoughts in these days of initiation.

By April I felt I was ready to make a trip back to the Continent to take up my acquaintanceship with André. I wrote him a short note and had an answer in about ten days. He said he would like to see me very much and he only regretted that the accommodation he had was insufficient to offer me a room. But he suggested that a pension, which I shall call Bastogne, in the town would look after me well. I wrote there to reserve a room and also to André to say that he could expect me before the end of the month.

I took the gold round to the bank in a small suit-case and the Van Eyck I put into the new case which I had made for it. This resembled the larder door and when hung in position appeared quite innocent. I locked the Minx away in a garage, packed up two suit-cases with clothes, note-books and folios of photographs, and set off for Belgium via train, boat and train.

The Pension Bastogne was on one side of a small square; cream-washed, red tiles on the door-step, polished and clean. The patron was pleasant and welcomed me as he showed me up to the room on the first-floor. This was simply furnished; almost bare boards, scrubbed near white; odd strips of thin carpet; a plain bed opposite the door; a pine-wood table; a hard-seat chair; a small chest of drawers; and a hanging-closet with a faded chintz curtain. A very ornate moulded glass lighting fitting hung down from the ceiling and a piece of near Art Nouveau posed as a bedside lamp. He told me that my dinner would be ready in thirty minutes and if there was anything I wanted extra, please let him know. I unpacked the cases I had brought with me, sorted out my books and the rest. After a wash and tidy I went down to the little dining-room.

There were only three other guests. Two of them I took to be a farmer and his wife either from the north of Belgium or Holland having a short break before the summer work. He was red faced with heavy-fingered hands; she was thick-set but with just traces of one of those early Flemish Madonnas who might have sat for Memling or Campin. The other occupant of the dining-room was small and dark and slim, with an air of the slicker about him; little black eyes revolved in their sockets, but he said nothing, made no sign to the other guests, just sat there quietly eating his way through course after course. As he finished, he wiped his mouth fastidiously and placed his knife and fork in an orderly position very carefully, then suddenly wisped out.

After my meal I enquired of the patron where I would find the address that André had given me. Following his instructions, I walked across the square and turned left and continued for about two hundred yards, turned right and left again, and then came to what appeared to be some sort of old warehouse. The large wooden doors were battened and barred across with a heavy rusted padlock. To the right of them was a small door inset above three steps and I could just make out André's name on a piece of yellowed card which had been fitted into a small metal slot. Beside this was a little pimple of a bell-push. I pressed it and could hear faintly at the top of the building a small tinny ringing which in its turn triggered off hurried steps across a floor and down some stairs. The door was opened and André was shaking my hand most warmly.

"Ah, Edward. It is wonderful to see you. Come up, mon ami." Together we climbed the stairs and at the top came into a small landing or hallway. André went on: "You will see what little I have here and how I cannot be polite enough to offer you a bed. This is my little kitchen with a bathroom through at the back. Here is my bedroom which I use also as a sitting-room." This room had a sloping ceiling and plain furniture which might have been made by the same hand as that which was in my room at the Bastogne. For heating there was an old beetle-type iron stove.

André led me from there into what was obviously his studio. This was a room about four times the size of the bedroom which was lit by a large north light and this he explained he had had put in specially. There were two large easels, a painting cabinet, and several tables. But most of all the impression I had was one of dedicated disorder.

There were bottles half-filled, bottles on their sides, bottles without corks, tubes of paint squeezed up without tops and half empty, brushes galore in jam jars, wine bottles, earthenware pots, palette knives, rags, saucers, plates, wooden palettes with paint on them, wooden palettes without paint on them. On one side of the room there was an immense book-case that went right up to the ceiling; it must have been all of twelve feet tall and about twenty-five feet long. In it hundreds of volumes, some fairly new, others with leather backs split and falling away; there were bundles of notes in their card folios pushed in on top of the books. On the wall beside this was another smaller set of shelves, and on these there were rows of glass-topped jars containing pigments, and more and more bottles of what I took to be varnishes, oils, solvents and other substances. Stacked on every available chair, cupboard-top and against the walls were canvases, panels and portfolios. The light was getting dim but it was strong enough to pick all this out and to feel the atmosphere of the place.

I must have been standing and gazing round for several minutes when I realized that André was in front of me and gazing into my eyes. He said:

"Edward, I am wondering what you think of my order or disorder? You see I think my order comes when I work on a picture on the easel. All round it may be what seems a terrible muddle to you; but I know where everything is, and if I don't have to bother about keeping tidy I can make the order in that picture in front of me."

"I am impressed, André. But I do hope you won't feel that I am going to impose on you for the next two weeks or so."

"Mon ami, sometimes I make what you call 'click' decisions. When we met in Brussels last June – O, it's nearly a year ago – I looked forward to having you here. I sensed with you, you are like myself, a devotee of the arts. I sensed that you wanted to know more; and anything, my friend, I can help you with I shall do."

He sat me down in a comfortable old basket-work chair and went to the kitchen and in a few minutes returned with coffee. Room was made for this on a table by sweeping a clear space with his hand and forearm. He reached into a small cupboard behind the table and pulled out a bottle of cognac. He offered me one of his little cigars, which I took, and we lit up. The coffee was poured out and a large cognac for me and a smaller one for himself, and then he said:

"Where do we begin?"

"André, I am ignorant of how paintings are really made. I should like to know how they are constructed; I want to find out about the materials, so that if I see a painting, perhaps I can appreciate more what is there."

"Well, Edward, this is a very big order. Where do we start? Do I take you to the flax fields where the material for the canvases is grown? Do I take you into the woods and we cut down a tree for the wooden panel? No, I am joking. There are so many ways in which artists have painted. Do you want me to demonstrate all the media? . . . The encaustic, as used in the mummy portraits in Egypt and again later in Greece, where the colours are put on with hot wax and manipulated with heated spatulas . . . Do you need right away to see how the frescoes work? . . . The buon with the damp plaster, the secco with dry . . . No, I think that we will work first on the main medium with which men have painted for so many years . . . oils."

In the next three weeks André took me through the material steps of painting that had been so sadly lacking and I believe still are from a study of the history of art. He not only talked, but also did. To illustrate small points of detail he would fumble amongst the piles and stacks of canvases and panels and pull out an example; generally, I might add, an original of the particular period he was talking about, and using his old-fashioned thick, heavy magnifying glass, he would explain to me how the painter or his apprentices had built up the underlying layers of gesso on the wood panel. Then he might point out to me details of the underpainting and drawing-in which could still be seen where the paint was thin. He further explained how a glaze had been applied to work with a colour underneath. He would indicate small areas of pentimento or ghosting through of earlier work, and would tell me how these had come about.

He took me through the principal details of restoration, demonstrating in detail the processes of transferring a painting from an old rotten panel or perished canvas on to a new support. On a little panel that had been at one time damp he pointed to where he had had to lay blisters with bees-wax and resin using a hot spatula, and told me why the blisters had come up; this was because the moisture had caused the sizing and priming to swell, thus forcing the paint film upwards.

Then with four different canvases which had been restored by someone else he showed me what to look for with over-retouching. With one of them, which had been painted about 1720, there was not a sign of a crack, even with his glass none could be seen. But when he placed the canvas under his microscope it became possible to note how the picture had not been just retouched; it had almost been one hundred per cent painted over, thus no cracks. He said it might look very pretty to some eyes, but where had its truth gone to? With the others there were small conceits on the part of the restorer; details over-emphasized, and here and there items had been added to disguise areas which had been over-skimmed during the restorer's work.

On the subject of cleaning he became most excited, telling me how so much damage could be done too easily. On one canvas he brought under a bright light he pointed to the mouth and eyes of the sitter and explained how too strong a solvent had been used by someone. The subtle glazes put on by the painter had been scrubbed away, giving the face a starved, weak, misty look.

Besides learning what I was after I discovered that I was learning about someone who was to become a very close friend indeed. André was a man who could in his own right paint the most exquisite landscapes, rather in the manner of Wouverman, developing at times a dramatic use of light and storm clouds, with dark heavy green trees dripping and soaked with moisture; he was also a man who had taught himself to be an accomplished restorer. In both his chosen fields he was a perfectionist as far as he could go, not only in what he did but also whom he did it for. I found that he chose his clients very carefully, whether they were those for whom he was restoring or those to whom he sold his pictures. This method may not have brought him great riches, but it brought him enough to live the way he wanted in peaceful seclusion away from arguments and publicity.

He had never married. His parents had died whilst he was still at school, and until he was thirty he had lived with a married sister whose husband was a local chemist. This had proved a happy arrangement because through the husband he had been able to get many of the materials he needed. When the chemist had died his sister had sold the business and moved to Antwerp to take up the position of housekeeper to one of the rich merchants there. Since then he had lived more or less as I found him now. Almost totally self-sufficient, he shopped and cooked for himself. Once a week Berthe from across the street would come in to put a brush and duster over as much of his little apartment as he would let her. André was now in his seventies and as happy as perhaps could be, inside his own little world. I found that, as far as I knew, he had no close friends, just a few acquaintances who would drink a glass of wine with us when we went down to the café sometimes late in the evenings. But apart from that, rather like myself André preferred to be alone.

Looking back now, it seems that I must have spent most of the next three years either staying in the Bastogne or travelling backwards and forwards to see André. It was nearly always by boat or train, but occasionally I would be profligate with a handful of petrol coupons. This had become easier because I had found out that if one visited the Continent some helpful character had decreed one could get at least three times the ration for such jaunts – and then there was always, at a price, the supplement from the 'black market'.

During these years I learnt most of what seemed necessary for me to know about the physical make-up of not only oil paintings, but also works in egg tempera, in gouache, also about water colours, back-glass paintings, and the intricate secrets of the miniature.

André even took me through methods of drawing and print-making, and I still have a small sketch of a flower he did when demonstrating silver-point. I had watched him prepare the paper with a thick wash of calcined bone powdered up and mixed with rabbit-skin glue; then, he had taken the silver point itself and put down the firm sensitive lines. At first these lines had been almost invisible, but after some days gradually the fine traces of silver which had been abraded off on the powdered bone tarnished, and the little drawing came to life with those warm sepia tones that are the charm of the medium. He indicated how it was possible to tell the difference between pastel and chalk, and wax and grease crayons, and showed me too the effect of over-fixing a pastel or charcoal drawing.

The ways and means of print production had, to a degree, been a bit of a jungle for me. I could tell a woodcut, which was done on the plank-grain, from a wood-engraving done on the end-grain. But on some of the other methods I was shaky. At the back of the studio behind the larger of the two easels André had a small press. With this and sundry copper and zinc plates he spent many hours showing me in the best way of all by actually doing the things in front of me.

Straightforward etching seemed fairly simple, with the grounding of the plate, the needling and then the acid bath. But aquatint was another story. André sprinkled the asphaltum powder on to the plate and then heated it until the asphaltum coalesced into thousands of tiny specks. Next he showed me how the subtle soft tonal effects could be produced. This was done by using stopping-out varnish applied over the lightest areas first, and then putting the plate into the acid, taking it out again with more stroking in of the varnish until the deepest tones had been reached.

Sugar-lift was one of those near magic arts. Some of the moderns had been experimenting with this, for it gave them a freedom and a method of printing that approached brushwork. For this technique André mixed a little glue, gamboge, lamp black and white sugar, making a paste with the consistency of cream. This he brushed into the design on the plate, and when it was dry he covered the surface with stopping-out varnish. When this had hardened he put the plate into a dish of water and it was left overnight. The next morning, in some strange way the water had got through the varnish and caused the sugary mixture to swell enough to lift off the varnish. This plate could then be eaten by the acid and printed in the ordinary way. I say ordinary way, but to me the printing of these intaglio methods was a messy business. First the ink would be rubbed over the surface of the plate, then it would be pushed well into the lines, and after that there would be a complicated wiping process, using coarse canvas, muslin and, last of all, generally the palm of the hand. The result of all this was that the artist could control, to some extent, the look of the final print.

From this we went through soft-ground etching; the metal engraving methods; and mezzotint with its mechanically textured plate, which is done using a weird instrument called a rocker, which has a series of small sharp teeth that will raise burrs on the plate surface. André showed me how the design was then worked with scrapers, burnishers and gravers to build up the picture. He discussed lithography and the stencil method of silk-screen. He produced from the bottom of a drawer a set of five wood-blocks that had been cut to produce a colour print. With these he was able to give me some idea of the sensitive control that a Japanese such as Hiroshige had commanded.

I think what fascinated me most was, one day on my third visit in mid-August of 1946, he let me accompany him on a painting expedition. We loaded ourselves with easel, paint box, panel, bag of odds and ends and a lunch basket. The scene he had chosen was not far from his studio; a trudge of less than a kilometre. Here was a sprawl of old farm-buildings, with their quaint arrangement of windows and doors. There were a few spartan stumpy trees, and in the foreground one of those meticulously husbanded fields in this part of that country. He had been preparing the wood panel he was going to work on for the previous two weeks, building up the traditional gesso of chalk and rabbit-skin glue, letting it harden and then sanding it smooth so that it looked and felt like polished ivory. Over this the evening before our excursion he had laid a veil or imprimatura of thin burnt umber in tempera. But now he had arrived at his chosen spot and he sat down on his little stool, eyeing the scene and then starting to lay it in with tempera, having mixed the pigments with just the pure fresh egg-yolk and a drop or two of linseed oil. The colours dried quickly in the open air and provided a stable ground for the oil painting which was to follow in the afternoon. I watched utterly absorbed. Here was someone who was totally involved in that mystic process of creativity. André was peering first at the landscape and then back to the panel; sitting back, once or twice even leaving his stool and walking away so that he could take a more distant look.

After we had had a simple snack of bread and cheese and two delicious pears, washed down with some rough red wine, he said:

"Now, that is the way many painters in the past would have laid in their work. On top I shall paint with the oils."

His technique and manner changed. He squeezed out on to his large palette quantities of paint from the various tubes in his box. I noticed that he was using really very few colours: white; bright yellow, possibly cadmium; yellow ochre; blue, cobalt; and, if I remember correctly, a green, either terre-verte or viridian; burnt umber; and light red.

I asked him: "Why don't you use more colours?"

He replied: "I have not yet been able to discover exactly what I can do with what I have here."

As he painted during the afternoon, it was a revelation. I thought what an almost incredible wealth of tints and tones he could raise with his knowledge and experience by mixing just those few lumps of paint round the edge of his palette. Slowly the little picture grew until by about seven o'clock in the evening to my eye it was almost finished. I can't remember what I said to him, but I know I showed great appreciation. But I do remember what he replied, which was:

"Edward, it is not quite finished. But tomorrow I shall put it on the easel in my studio and I shall look just what has to be done; and then, Edward, the next time you come back it will be dry and I shall have a frame for it and it will be yours."

I still have that panel. It only measures about ten inches by about fourteen, but to me it is one of the most precious things I have managed to keep.

The next morning I sat beside him drinking a cup of coffee and watching him as he looked and looked and looked. Possibly, I think, he may only have put in about a dozen strokes, but those little flicks of colour fell into place and locked the whole into success.

*　　*　　*

It was early March 1947 and I was planning yet another of my trips to André when I started thinking the time might be getting ripe for the disposal of the Van Eyck. The gold I felt I would hang on to for the time being, and did eventually sell it reasonably well about nine months later.

The celebrated panel had spent a long time disguised as a larder door. I had had the stray peep to see if all was well, and it had been well. I had looked out the address of the dealer in Alsace whom I had overheard the men discussing about a year and a half previously, and I had thought around the problem of camouflage for the trip through Customs. The approach I had decided upon was slightly unorthodox. I made up what to all intents and purposes was a rather thick hollow drawing-board. The Van Eyck was a bit over four feet long and somewhat less than two feet wide, a rather awkward shape. Being slim, however, it would fit into this new disguise comfortably. On the top of the 'fake' drawing-board I stretched a large sheet of heavy Whatman smooth drawing-paper. Using what skill I could bring to play from earlier days and with the help of tracing-paper, I drew in a wide panoramic view of Bruges. The operation, I must say, occasioned an undue amount of effort, but the final product complete with some preliminary washes of colour would answer for the work of some minor artistic luminary on his way back to complete a commission, I hoped. I also had with me a convincing array of water-colour tubes, brushes, rags, china palettes, sponges and other gear. The drawing-board fitted easily into the back of the Minx, and I was off down the Dover road.

When I finally tracked down the Alsatian dealer's place, it was in a somewhat unsuspected quarter of the town. There was no posh shop-fronted gallery; in fact, there was no sign of vulgar commerce at all. If it hadn't been for the name of the street, I wouldn't have found it. The house was stone and dark slate set back and standing alone in a square of garden that had been almost entirely given over to thick evergreen shrubs. These shrubs completely shrouded the entrance and hid the front door from the street and the neighbours. I drove cautiously into the small drive, and turning, parked just past the porch. I got out and was about to pull the bell-chain when the front door swung open and in the dim light I could make out a shortish figure.

"What do you want? This is a private house," a rather crackly voice asked me.

"Excuse me, Mr (and I mentioned his name), but I have been told you are interested in early German and Flemish panel paintings."

"Sometimes I might be. Who are you? Where are you from? You are English."

"I am someone who may have something of interest for you, which I might be prepared to sell."

He pulled the door wider and said:

"All right. But I have only a few minutes to spare. Bring it in."

I pulled the drawing-board out of the back of the Minx and followed him into the hall and then into what appeared to be his study, which was heavily curtained and lit only by two shaded reading lamps, one over the desk and the other over a form of salon easel.

"Come on then, let me see it," he barked.

I must admit that Mr Dealer was not quite what I had imagined he would be. Still, people very rarely are. He stood about five feet six. A rather long head with indrawn cheeks and a wisp of sucked moustache under an over-large nose held washy grey eyes close up under rather busy eyebrows. He had a nervous trick of pulling and massaging his fingers and kept up an almost continuous clearing of his throat.

I flicked off the securing catches at the end of the drawing-board and slid out the Van Eyck. Hardly before it had come clear, the voice came on again:

"Ah . . . Ah . . . Ah . . . I wondered when it would turn up. You want to sell this?"

"If your offer is right."

"You know what this is?"

"Of course."

I could see with his increased agitation that he was in a struggle as to what he could, should or would do. He could try bluster and threats of police. But I didn't think that he would. Greed was already showing in the corners of his mouth and eyes. He took the panel from me and turned it over, then taking a small glass from a waistcoat pocket, he peered for a few seconds at the top right-hand corner of the back of the panel. He turned it round again and placed it on the easel, after which he stood back about a yard and one could sense the appetite of the man for gain seeping out of him. Suddenly he turned:

"Who sent you to me? Was it (he mentioned three or four household names in the art business)?"

"Does it make any difference?" I responded.

"No I suppose not. I will give ten thousand dollars."

I didn't bother to reply but went over to the easel and took the panel and was about to put it back in the drawing-board when he said:

"Wait a minute, let us have a drink and work things out."

He went over to a small cabinet and opening it took out a bottle of whisky, and was about to take out a large glass when I saw him half turn his head, replace it and take down two smaller tumblers. He brought these and the bottle over to a small table and pointed me to a chair. After having poured out two pretty miserable Scotches, he turned to me again:

"What have you in your mind?"

"You know your prices as well as I do. The last three Van Eycks sold were all into six figures – pounds sterling –: the Hermitage 'Annunciation', and the 'Three Maries' – that was the one Goering was after, which went to the Boymans. The Philadelphia Museum puts their 'St Francis' in the same bracket."

"Yes, but this is only a part of a work. Who is going to be interested in this by itself?"

"I know exactly what it is. By the way, you are forgetting the 'Annunciation' was also just a part of a triptych. Andrew Mellon gave over £100,000 some time before the war for that, and it's now in the National Gallery Washington. That was painted about the same time as this and there is little difference value-wise."

"You are trying to push me. It is a fine piece. I have a patron who I know wants it."

"That is simple then; you know what you can ask your man to pay you for it; you know your profit margin; so . . . ," I shrugged my shoulders.

"I have not met you before in the trade. I will go to twenty-five thousand dollars."

"If you want it that bad, you had better think again."

The bartering went on for about five minutes. I guessed that he knew that I knew what he was going to make on the deal. Eventually I managed to screw him higher than I had hoped. As we agreed on the figure, I could see strange reactions wriggling away under the skin on his face. Greed can bring on frantic mental indigestion.

"All right, my friend. In notes." As he said it, he was unable to hide a leer of satisfaction at the thought of an easy profit to come.

Soon I was on my way, two small whiskies and a comforting thick wad of greenbacks to the profit side. I didn't like the district, so I drove some fifty miles further south before I stopped for the night.

The next morning at a deserted lay-by I tore up my drawing of Bruges and effectively smashed the packing-case, putting the remnants into a waste-bin. I then drove into Switzerland and stowed those lovely dollars away under the solid protection of just a string of numbers in a bank. Enough there to keep me in reasonable comfort for several years.

In less than forty-eight hours I was once again with André. During the times we were together, not every moment was spent discussing techniques and materials. We ranged over the whole field. One aspect that was to be useful to me he seemed very well-informed on. This was the copyist. This is by no means an innovation of the present day – far from it. In fact, as I learnt from talking to André and indeed as I have found out to a greater extent since, the practices of copy making of famous pictures and painting in the manner of great painters have been rife since the fifteenth century.

André stressed how the copyist either innocently or by design can cause a good deal of confusion and trouble. As time passes the problem of authenticating a painting can become increasingly difficult, if, for example, it is three or four hundred years old. As a good instance of what went on with this kind of thing, André took Raphael, who in his own time drew numerous copyists and imitators. Even some of those who worked in close association with him may have made a profit out of it; for instance, there was Guilio dei Giannuzzi, at times called Giulio Pippi, but more generally Giulio Romano. He was born in Rome about 1492, and at a young age was apprenticed to Raphael, being also one who assisted the master with his work in the Vatican, and indeed many consider him amongst the greatest of Raphael's pupils. He copied a number of Raphael's Madonnas, also executed in his master's manner some of Raphael's designs. When Raphael died, in his will he left all his studio equipment to Giulio Romano and Gianfrancesco Penni, who were his executors, and he instructed them that they should finish his incomplete frescoes in the Sala di Constantino in the Vatican.

The works of Raphael also attracted the attentions of a Flemish painter some time after the master's death. Jan Gillis Delcour, who was born around 1632 near Liege, studied with Geraert Douffet. Later he travelled to Rome, where he worked under Andrea Sacchi and Carlo Maratti. Whilst in Rome it is recorded that he made excellent copies of many of Raphael's best works.

Travelling round Europe, one comes across a Spaniard

bent on the same track. Juan Bautista del Mazo was born in Madrid about 1610. He studied in the school of Velasquez, whose daughter he married. In his own right he must have had considerable talent because he succeeded his father-in-law as court painter to Philip IV in 1661. Palomino praises him equally for his painting of portraits, history pieces, landscapes, hunting scenes, seascapes and views of towns. But Mazo also had an out-of-the-ordinary talent for copying, not only the works of Raphael, but also those of Tintoretto, Titian and Veronese. The King himself used him to copy the Venetian pictures in his collection, which task Mazo did so well that it was only apparently with difficulty that the copies could be distinguished from the originals.

Advancing across the map, and more than a hundred years later, one finds Nikolai Abraham Abilgaard, who was born at Copenhagen in 1743. His father was an artist and he taught his son, who after his apprenticeship travelled to Italy and spent most of his time in Rome, where he too latched on to Raphael and, for good measure, also Michelangelo and Titian. In 1777 he returned to his native earth, and in 1786 was made a professor of the Academy, and director of this body in 1802. Crunch point with him could be that, in 1794 there was a fire at the Christianburg Palace where his work was stored and the historian records that some of the best pieces were destroyed. The archives are vague, for it does not seem to be known how many works he brought back from Italy, how many were in the Palace, or indeed how many were saved from the flames or the whereabouts of any that were.

I discussed at length this matter of copying with André and asked him,

"When you have a copyist who is a contemporary of the master he is copying or imitating, and who has access to the same canvas, panels, pigments, brushes, everything that the man uses he is aping, how can you be certain that the work; for example, by one of those just mentioned is a copy by him or is, again for example, a genuine Raphael?''

André thought for a long time, and then he went to his book-case and pulled out one or two folios and fumbled through their contents, finally producing some photographs which would illustrate the points he wished to make, he replied:

"This thing you have asked me, Edward, I would think is the one that troubles the dealers and the collectors more than any other. How can one be sure of the provenance of a painting which is three or four hundred years old? During that time it will have been in perhaps many collections, through many dealers' hands. Most likely it will have been restored, perhaps even heavily repainted. Unfortunately there are really not many paintings of quality which have behind them a life story that has not a question mark anywhere, and with many one can find that some scholar at some time or another has tilted a doubt or cast an aspersion at them. For myself, I like to look; for, after all is said and done, if the copyist has used the same canvas and paints as the man he is copying or imitating, chemistry is not going to be much help, nor are other scientific methods of examination. What I am going to say now may sound a little up in the air but, generally speaking, the longer you look at a copy the more the strength of it will fall; the longer you look at an original the more the truth of the artist comes out. Truth is a strange thing in painting; it is something that is perhaps laughed at. Look here. In my right hand I have a photo of a 'Madonna' by Raphael; in my left a photo of the copy by Giulio Romano. At first glance there does not seem anything in it. But a little study slowly shows some indefinable lack of confidence, a shade less purity of – what can I say – these things are nuances so slight that they go past nearly all eyes. Now think of a landscape by Hobbema, a painting by Michelangelo such as the unfinished 'Entombment' in your National Gallery, a landscape by Monet; these all have that feeling of truth which is very difficult for the copyist to achieve.

André paused as if giving the matter more thought, and then continued:

(I did not say anything because I did not wish to interrupt his flow of thought.)

"Yes, and trouble can come when a collector is not able to make a comparison between an original and what is really a copy. And then again, many of the copyists, particularly in the earlier centuries, were extremely capable artists in their own right."

My friend had set me off on a track that was going to take a lot of researching into to ferret out where the real began and ended. I must admit that until I had spoken with him that day I had had no idea how wide-spread this business of copying had been and how much even the innocent side of it had been abused. Signatures had been added, pictures swirled around through the dealers and the international sales rooms until museums, galleries and collectors kept finding themselves with having been sold a pup. It is perhaps the diversity of the copyist which makes him so difficult in many cases to pick up, and also – as André and I had discussed – there was this point that if he had been imitating or copying a contemporary of his it was simplicity itself to use the same materials. Indeed this is one of the hardest nuts the forger has to try and crack when he is working a long time after his target-artist worked.

When I returned to London the next time I therefore read in the libraries, borrowed or bought pretty well every relevant book I could get hold of which might give me some assistance with my quest of trying to sort out who did what and when it was done. I soon found that my investigations were disclosing some quite remarkable facts and characters. They seemed to be almost legion. And the details that came to light proved more and more fascinating.

A good example of a painter with considerable quality fogging the field is Giovanni Antonio Bazzi, or de' Bazzi, often miscalled Razzi, but generally known now as Sodoma. He was born in 1477 at Vercelli in Piedmont. His training started when he was thirteen with a glass-maker Martino Spanzotti; this lasted for seven years, after which the young Sodoma came under the thrall of Leonardo da Vinci in Milan, and it can be noted by looking at the works of Sodoma how very strongly he was affected by the individuality of his master. He did, however, fall foul of Vasari, the painter, architect and biographer (born in 1511), and best recalled for his 'Lives of the Most Eminent Painters, Sculptors and Architects'), who in a number of places makes it quite evident that he had little use for Sodoma, although in justice he does praise him sometimes. He made up jealous and malicious stories about him, of which a large number can be proved untrue. Amongst other things Vasari complained that the artist was wasting too much of his time after his first arrival in Milan in making drawings from sculptures, particularly those of the great Giacomo della Quercia including those on the celebrated Fonta Gaia in the Piazzo del Campo. Eventually the output of Sodoma starts to move away from the public gaze into the twilight; for example, practically all the works that are recorded as being painted by him during this early period seem either to have been destroyed or to have disappeared. In 1536, when he was a mature painter, it is recorded that he was visiting and working for his patron and friend James V, Prince of Piombino, though for this period none of his works can now be definitely identified. In 1540 he went on a visit to Lorenzo di Galeotto dei Medici at Volterra, but the sole trace I could find of his labours whilst there was the figure of the Infant Christ inserted by him in Signorelli's 'Circumcision', which is now in the National Gallery, London. More complicated still for the provenance hound after this quarry is the fact that Sodoma had himself numerous followers, imitators and ones who copied him. Added to all this, besides having a talent for painting, Sodoma had too a rare gift for drawing, and there have been many incidents where Raphael's, Da Vinci's and his drawings have become confused, with some experts giving cross attributions. Another small point about the influence of Leonardo on Sodoma is that, in a number of his pictures areas have become disfigured and darkened from an unwise choice of pigments. This defect occurred in the foreground of Leonardo's 'Virgin of the Rocks', which is also in the National Gallery in London. It must have been that Leonardo himself could have had no idea that there would be such a noticeable colour change with the paints he was using for the plants in this part of the painting.

The Renaissance must have been such a moment of sheer creative ebullience that some of the boys almost let it run away with them. There was the Florentine goldsmith and engraver Baccio Baldini, contemporary of Botticelli, with whom, according to a number of writers, he worked in conjunction. Baldini seemingly led a life in the half-light, because, apart from the facts mentioned above, scarcely anything is known about him except that he flourished in Florence from about 1460 to 1485. A good deal of confusion is possible over his works and Botticelli's, as both worked in the same manner and neither of them used signatures or monograms.

To the north, in the Netherlands, we find that there was

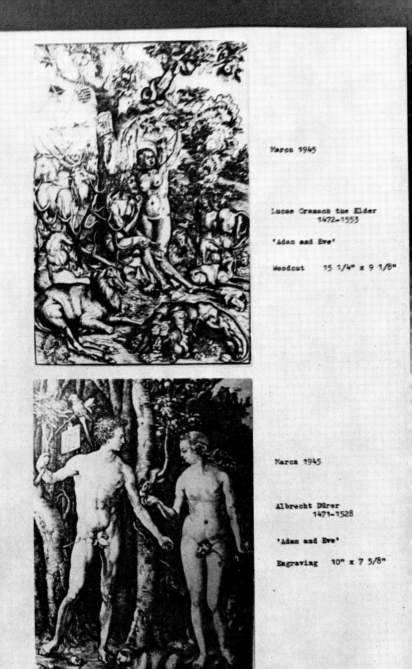

March 1945

Lucas Cranach the Elder
1472-1553

'Adam and Eve'

Woodcut   15 1/4" x 9 1/8"

March 1945

Albrecht Dürer
1471-1528

'Adam and Eve'

Engraving   10" x 7 5/8"

Page from record file of 1945.

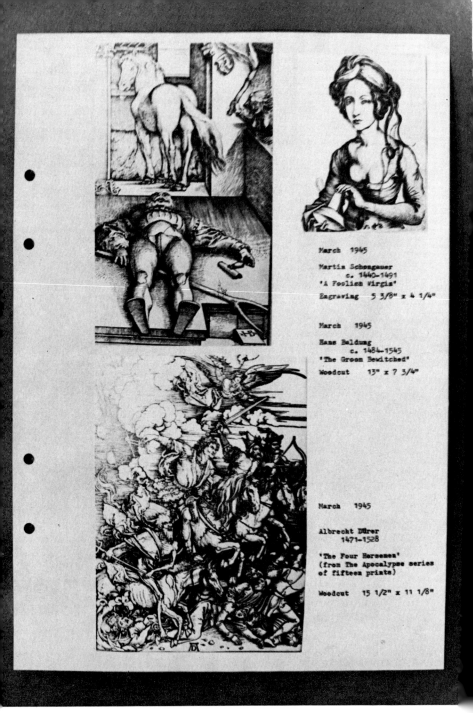

March 1945

Martin Schongauer
        c. 1440-1491
'A Foolish Virgin'
Engraving 5 3/8" x 4 1/4"

March 1945

Hans Baldung
        c. 1484-1545
'The Groom Bewitched'
Woodcut   13" x 7 3/4"

March 1945

Albrecht Dürer
        1471-1528

'The Four Horsemen'
(from The Apocalypse series
of fifteen prints)

Woodcut 15 1/2" x 11 1/8"

Another page from 1945, first year of operations.

1963

Francisco Goya
1746-1828

'Tantalus'
(from the series
The Caprices)

Etching and Aquatint
7 1/4" x 5"

1963

Giovanni Battista Piranesi
1720-1778

'The Prisons'

Etching   21 1/2" x 16 1/4"

Two etchings from the record file for 1963.

'Nature morte aux pommes et aux raisins' by Paul Gauguin.
Stolen 1970, with 'Two chairs . . .' by Bonnard. (see next photograph section.)

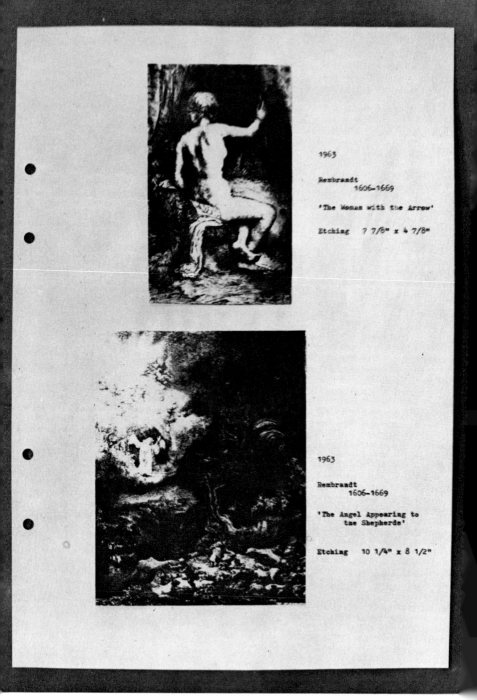

1963

Rembrandt
      1606-1669

'The Woman with the Arrow'

Etching 7 7/8" x 4 7/8"

1963

Rembrandt
      1606-1669

'The Angel Appearing to
    the Shepherds'

Etching 10 1/4" x 8 1/2"

Two Rembrandt etchings from the record file.

August 1974

David Teniers the
          Younger
1610-1690

'Rocky Landscape
        with Figures'

Oil   16" x 26"

August 1974

Jan Wynaats
    1615-1679

'Landscape'

Oil :   16" x 20"

August 1974

Jacob van Ruisdael
    c. 1625-1682

'Landscape with
        Traveller'

Oil   21" x 18"

Record file page for 1974.

Specimen artists' watermarks on papers for drawings, water colours etc. *Left* – Rubens; Jan II Brueghel; van Bloemen; Siberechts. *Right* – Jordaens; van Dyke; Savery; David II Teniers.

William de Poorter, who lived in Haarlem, and who was apparently a pupil of Rembrandt's. He seems to have flourished around 1630 to 1645, and to have had the enviable ability of being able to simulate to a degree the almost magical control of light, half-tones and shade of his master.

The skilled copyist crops up all over Europe. Such works cannot be confined to a particular time or to any school of painters. It was the bewildering number of instances that I felt was eating away at my confidence in even attempting to authenticate any that I was particularly interested in. At this point I was still concentrating on what I termed the copyist as quite separate from the outright forger. I was to explore the latter's field more fully later on.

Meanwhile, amongst those I was busy tracking down now, I came across Cesare Dalle Ninfe, a Venetian who was working around 1590 to 1600, and who was one of the cleverest imitators of Tintoretto. It is recorded that Ninfe had a similar inventiveness, facility of brush and colour controls as characterize the Venetian master. In Venice also was Girolamo Dante, known as well as Girolamo di Tiziano, this latter because he spent some time as assistant to the great one. His output appears to be confined to the period of 1550 to 1580, and it was said that those of his pictures which were retouched by Titian would slide past even very skilled connoisseurs; and so who is to be sure that some of his own complete works did not get hooked on to the band-waggon.

On a lesser scale, in the nineteenth century, there was John Birch, who was a landscape painter, and who was born at Norton in Derbyshire, in 1807. His early career was spent on a somewhat deadening occupation, that of assisting his father as a file-cutter. After this he went to a carver and gilder, and then later travelled to London, where he studied

6—MOAAT * *

under Henry Perronet Briggs. Whilst he was in this studio he actually received commissions to paint copies of portraits which had been done by his master. He was so successful that again it was difficult to distinguish the copy from the original.

Still in England, and working also in the nineteenth century, I came across a gentleman B. Blake — not to be confused with the earlier William. This B. Blake was in his own right a minor painter of birds, fish and still life, but he was also a spendthrift and inclined to hurry his work and often to repeat compositions. Nevertheless he had the luck to strike a popular vein, but he fell subject to the dealer belt, for not only did they employ minor hacks to copy his work, but, finding also that he himself had a talent for copying, they set him to produce imitations of Dutch painters, which he apparently did so well that these opportunists were able to mislead their customers.

Back on the Continent, there was, I found, the individual Pieter Nason, born early in the seventeenth century in Amsterdam or possibly the Hague. He certainly became a member of the Hague Guild of Painters, and in 1656 was one of the forty-seven members who established the 'Pictura' Society. He, I found also, had had a dirty one dealt him. A manuscript by Pieter Terwesten makes it not unlikely that Nason studied with Jan van Ravesteyn. It is believed that the name of Nason was removed from a number of his own paintings which have since been attributed not only to his master Ravesteyn, but also to Mierevelt, and Moreelse.

From the same period comes Adriaan Hanneman — also from the Hague and a pupil of Ravesteyn. He got himself tied up with Van Dyck. Noting the encouragement given to the arts by Charles I, he visited England soon after Van Dyck and found his talents quickly got him work. Indeed during some sixteen years he spent in England he painted a number of portraits of the nobility and others, in which work he greatly improved his style by imitating that of Van Dyck. When the civil war broke out he returned to Holland and lived at the Hague, where he was court painter to Mary Princess of Orange, and in 1665 he became director of the Academy.

As one scans the history of art, one is led to the inescapable conclusion that a great many of them were at it one way or another. The gifted son of Frans Hals, Frans Hals the Younger, painted portraits and still life; sometimes he copied the works of his father and sometimes imitated him. Reynier Hals, also a son of Frans the Elder, may have been a somewhat mediocre hand at 'genre' subjects, but it is likely that a number of his works have, over the years, been passed across the counter under the name of his uncle Dirk.

Back again in Italy I came across a really startling one. Andrea d'Agnolo, better known as Andrea del Sarto, was born in Florence in 1486. In earlier references he can also be found miscalled Vannucchi. Giovanni Cinelli (writing in 1677) seems to be the first to call him by that name. This mistake happened apparently because of a misreading of Andrea's monogram of two A's for an A and a V. His full name, if one wants to go into it, was Andrea d'Agnolo di Francesco di Luca di Paolo del Migliore, which probably accounted for the fact that he was inclined to use a monogram. Quite apart from being a quality painter Del Sarto had an outstanding ability to imitate and copy the works of other masters. He had an accuracy which sometimes even deceived the masters themselves. Vasari notes down a remarkable incident which he himself saw. Raphael – one way or another I seemed to keep coming across him – had painted for the Cardinal Giulio de' Medici, who was afterwards Pope Clement VII, the portrait of Leo X, seated between that prelate and Cardinal Rossi, the background having been put in by Giulio Romano (whom we have met earlier). Federigo II, Duke of Mantua, when passing through Florence had seen this picture and asked Clement VII to give it to him. The Pope thereupon gave directions to Ottaviano de' Medici to send the portrait to Mantua. But Ottaviano was unwilling that Florence should be deprived of this treasure and so got Del Sarto to make a copy, which was sent instead to the Duke of Mantua, who at this time had Giulio Romano in his service. Romano, not suspecting the deception, was completely satisfied that it was the original, and it wasn't until Vasari told him that he had actually seen the copy being made and pointed to the private mark of Del Sarto that Romano could believe it was so.

As one goes on reading up the past, it becomes blatantly obvious that misdemeanours and outright chicanery are far from being the special prerogative of the twentieth century, although certain circles are today probably doing quite nicely by adding to the list of discrepancies. I was to go on finding more and more examples wherever I went.

Pieter de Ryng, a Flemish painter who was working in the middle of the seventeenth century, mainly on still life, reveals in his pictures the ability to simulate the textures, tints and tones of such things as oysters, fruit, platters, metals, and glass vessels. Several of his works were brought to England by dealers, who then found they couldn't sell them under his name, so promptly changed it to Jan Davidz de Heem. Perhaps more enlightened merchants in some cases may have changed it back again.

Another reason for query and outright worry for the collector, the scholar and the rest is when history records fire, earthquake or iconoclasm. There may be the bald assumption that the work of an artist or part of it is destroyed. But how sure can we be of this destruction? In the general commotion pictures may be been removed and hidden for a period; they may have travelled around; they may have been altered or re-signed with another signature.

The search took me deeper and farther and farther afield. In Germany I tracked down August Wilhelm Julius Ahlborn, who was born at Hanover in 1796, and who received some instructions from Wach in Berlin. In 1827 he went to Italy to complete his education. He seems to have stayed put there for some thirty years but every now and then sent pictures to Berlin, and apparently whilst on a trip back to Germany, in 1833, was elected a member of the Berlin Academy. It is known that whilst in Italy he produced religious pictures after Fra Angelico, Perugino, and other early Italian painters. It can be presumed therefore that the possibility exists of such 'after' pictures being mixed up with those he sent back to Germany. And in time, who knows what may have happened to them.

Amongst the names of the increasing number who were arousing my interest was that of Antonello D'Antonio (or Degli Antonj), much better known as Antonello da Messina. I could find few authentic details of his life. He was born at Messina in the middle of the fifteenth century (exact date varied with the writer) amd received some art instruction in Sicily. Later he went to Naples, where he saw in the collection of Alfonso of Aragon a painting by Jan van Eyck. This so impressed him that he adopted a similar manner. There are stories about him travelling to the north of Europe to study further the work of the Van Eycks, but now these are considered unlikely to be true. The Van Eycks have often been credited with the invention of oil painting, but this too is incorrect; what they really painted in was a mixed media; they alike with people such as Dürer, Altdorfer and Grünewald were using a variation of egg tempera, and it was from this that the medium of oils was to evolve. It could be that part of the credit could be given to Messina, as has been actually done by a number of writers since his time. It was owing to Messina that the Venetian painters were led to the freedom that oils can give. Pigments mixed with egg-yolk, as with tempera, tend to dry out almost bland and lacking in strength, whilst these same pigments mixed with oils at once take on a richness and power. Another advantage is that when painting with oils it is an easy matter to estimate how the colours will look when they have dried and have been varnished. With tempera this is difficult because the application of varnish can bring about considerable changes in tone and colour. Blues, browns and other dark colours are especially affected. It is considered certain that Antonello visited Venice in the period 1473–6, where he painted a 'Madonna & St. Michael', in San Cassiano, which is now lost. The word 'lost' seems to have many connotations when applied to works of art.

As the conglomeration of information grew, it damn nearly put me off. It's one thing to make a boggle-de-botch at an auction or be duped by a dealer if you are a connoisseur or a director of a gallery. It is quite another thing if you go and remove a painting supposedly by a well-known name and you pass it on for a suitably large remuneration to the next owner whom you may have chosen or who may have chosen you to carry out the commission for him. Should he find that all he has is some old copy worth a mere fraction, with some of the people I deal with in this particular trade, the world would very soon shrink as he or his came after me. So I felt constrained to continue my studies.

I had not previously come across a gentleman called Cesare Aretusi. He was active in the latter half of the sixteenth century in Bologna, but he has since then, I should think, caused some bewilderment, to put it mildly. He worked in conjunction with Giambattista Fiorini and between them they produced a number of paintings of considerable merit. Aretusi himself must have had a touch of the fairies, because it is recorded that at will he could assume the style of almost any painter and be able to pass off these imitations as originals. One master whom he was notably successful with was Correggio, an artist who has great rarity value and has been much sought after; in fact, Aretusi was given a commission to copy Correggio's 'Notte' for the Church of San Giovanni in Parma. Anton Raffael Mengs, the German painter who had been brought up by his father (court painter of Dresden) on the models of Correggio and Raphael and the like, and who in 1762 wrote a treatise on Beauty in Painting, when he saw this replica by Aretusi, declared that if by chance the original were lost, it could very well be replaced unnoticeably by the copy.

Not long ago an acquaintance of mine bought a painting by Van Dyck, or could it have been really by Adriaan de Lelie, who was born at Tilburgen in 1755, or might it have been by Jean Eugène Charles Alberti, who was born in Amsterdam in 1781? Both these men were highly talented copyists and imitators of Van Dyck. If one digs deep enough, there are a great many others who aped that artist.

When matters get really complicated is when you find a family having a go at it. There were the Dutch kinsmen the Van de Veldes, and perhaps even more so the Danish family of Alken, who had settled in England, and who specialized in sporting pictures and prints. The production of this lot starts with Sefferin Alken (1717–82) and then goes on with Henry Gordon Alken, who died in 1894. Sefferin had a son Samuel, who had four sons, Sam, George, Sefferin and

Henry. This Henry had two sons, Henry and Sefferin. This last Henry was actually christened Samuel Henry but was called Henry Gordon. The crux is that all the Alkens painted in the same style and signed the resulting products S or H Alken. The last Henry did sign some H Alken, Junior, but he also is known to have passed off some paintings as being by his father, whose work was a good deal better than his own (one simple device he used for this was just to omit the 'Junior'.)

There is also the family of Apshoven and they must have caused art historians some tooth-sucking. There were two brothers: Thomas, who has been miscalled Theodor, and Ferdinand – some authorities have even given the opinion that in fact these two were one and the same man! As regards the spelling of the family's surname, sometimes it is as above, but it can also be Abshoven or Abtshoven. Taking a look at part of the genealogical tree of this clan, who practised their art in Antwerp in the sixteenth and seventeenth centuries, I saw there were: Ferdinand I, Ferdinand II, then Thomas, and parallel with him Ferdinand III; from the union of Thomas one got Ferdinand IV; and from that of Ferdinand III came a Willem. One writer, Waagen, brings in a Michael whom no one else seems to mention. Ferdinand I was baptized in Antwerp in 1576, later he studied with Adam van Noort. By 1597 he had been made free of the Guild of Painters, and he was reputed to be an historian and a portrait painter of note. But crunch point here – no work by him seems to exist. Ferdinand the Younger, thought to be brother of the more celebrated Thomas, studied with Teniers the Younger. In 1657 he was admitted to the Antwerp Guild as a Master's son. Some twenty years later he was offered the position of Dean to that body. At this stage I really reached for the ice-bag. Comment was made that the paintings of both this

Ferdinand – the trick I found was to get the right one –
and Thomas greatly resembled those of Teniers under
whose name apparently many of them have slipped by.

Prime confusion probably best reigns with the name De
Vos. There are a number of painters called this, practically
all of them congregating in the sixteenth and seventeenth
centuries, although to assist in the general mental maze,
painters with the name have also continued in Holland
right through to this century. They come from a variety of
families, but most of them painted the same subjects; that
is, landscapes, portraits, and animals.

Cornelis de Vos was born at Hulst about 1585, but
early in the seventeenth century there is another Cornelis De Vos who was no relation to the first one.
Lambertus de Vos from Mechlin was working in the
sixteenth century, and a little earlier in the same century
came Marten de Vos from Antwerp, himself the son of an
artist (Pieter) who had been received into the Academy at
Antwerp in 1519. Marten had a son, also Marten, who
became a painter, and who was also born at Antwerp; and
father Marten also had a brother called Pieter, who had a
son called Willem. Then there is Paulus, the brother of the
first Cornelis mentioned. And in the seventeenth century
too came a Jan. Rounding off this catalogue for this period
there is Simon de Vos (born at Antwerp in 1603) who
studied in the school of Rubens, and who on occasion has
had some of his altar-pieces mistaken for those of Rubens.
Apart from the foregoing diatribe, there are writers who
murmur about a further Pieter, and Willem, and Hendrik,
as well as the possibility of even more Christian names.
This adds up to what one might call an art dealer's dozen
of De Voses all around the same time, all painting away like
mad at the same subjects, and all conveniently misted away
behind the velvet curtains of art history. In a recent London

sale there was a 'Madonna and Child with Saint Joseph, in a wooded landscape' on a panel. The painter was given as 'C. de Vos', whether it was one of the Cornelises or some other De Vos who had turned up to join in the game, who knows?

For the provenance prover, there is another snag; many artists in the sixteenth and seventeenth centuries at times seemed to work on the commune principle when producing their pictures. Probably the studio of Rubens epitomizes this the best of all. The master surrounded himself with a star-studded team of talent, one or other of whom could be called in to add his bit. The theme can be further illustrated by the gentleman Joos (Jodocus) de Momper, who was born in Antwerp in 1564. He was the son of Bartholomeus de Momper, a picture dealer who may also have been an amateur artist himself, and who may have taken part in the early education of his son. Joos apparently entered the Guild of St Luke in 1581 and by 1611 had become Dean. One finds his works frequently decorated with areas by Jan 'Velvet' Brueghel, Frans Francken, Teniers the Elder and Van Balen. Tricky situations can emerge with some of these joint efforts and it can often depend on fashion or which artist at the time is thought the most notable or valuable as to which name such pictures will be publicized under.

Somewhere about 1619 or 1620 at either Utrecht or Schoonhoven there was born Hendrik Naeuwincx or with a secondary spelling Naiwinck. He was a contemporary of the celebrated Jan Asselyn who very kindly was wont to put figures and animals into the landscapes of Naeuwincx, so sowing seeds of confusion for today that these paintings could be by Asselyn rather than largely by the lesser hand. A side issue in this case is, in the 17th century there lived in Hamburg a landscape painter Nauinx or Navinx whose work at times is mixed up with that of Naeuwincx; and

Nauinx (or Navinx) also had his private home-help who put in figures, one J. M. Weyer.

As I still raked around in this area, I came across Nicaise Bernaerd, born in 1608. At a suitable age he went to study with Frans Snyders. Bernaerd's work, shall I say strangely enough, has a strong resemblance to that of Snyders, and it is quite certain that Bernaerd's paintings have been sold as genuine productions of the greater master, no doubt by what might be termed a scholastic error in authentification.

I managed to extricate myself from this labyrinth, at any rate for the time being, before I became too dazed, and, as it was already autumn, set off for Belgium. André welcomed me as always, and I hadn't been with him very long when we were deep in more talks about the snares with collecting.

"Edward," he said, "you have been reading the papers about this Van Meegeren case? It is tearing holes in the prophets and know-it-alls."

"Yes, André. You know, I remember reading an article in the Burlington Magazine a couple of years before the war about the finding of a new Vermeer. The article by Abraham Bredius was giving a terrific write-up to 'Christ and the Disciples at Emmaus', then claimed as an unknown painting by a great master – i.e. Vermeer."

André and I remembered that it had been in July 1945 that Han van Meegeren, who had been imprisoned on a charge of collaborating with the enemy, in that he had sold a picture pertaining to be by Vermeer to Goering, had suddenly broken silence and claimed that not only was he the painter of this 'Vermeer', but also of other works claimed to be by that artist, and by Frans Hals and Pieter de Hooch.

Now, as André said, the resulting upheaval was involving many people including not only legal authorities, but also a number of top scientists concerned with artistic research in their laboratories. He went on:

"This is in many ways a bad business. I feel sorry, for instance, for Paul Coremans. He is someone I have met once or twice and whom I admire. He has been the one who has done so much to uncover these frauds. And what is happening now? There is argument. Maybe there will be persecution . . . and poor Coremans? The whole business of this Van Meegeren man is extraordinary. He is not like the people we were discussing earlier, those copyists. Here is a man who they say has something bitter inside. And then, you see Edward, he didn't in the real sense set out to imitate Vermeer exactly, but to paint in a manner in which Vermeer could have been expected to paint during a period of his life when there is a gap in his production. He knew the great critics were forecasting that religious subjects by Vermeer might one day be found. So, egged on by what one cannot really be sure of, he produced such works for these men. But this whole business is a harmful one for the arts, and it largely comes about because of collectors with too much money and not enough pictures. So, artists, sometimes of great skill, fall and they supply the pictures. But here again, the forger is not a new person, he is way back in history; although, I must say, the artists today, at least a good many of them, seem to make it very easy for the forger. He can get the paper and canvas and other materials, and their techniques are becoming in some cases so easy to fake. I feel sure there must be several people who are making good money right now with these men of this century. But the trouble again is for the collector; even if and when these practitioners are exposed, how can anybody be really sure that all the fraud works have been swept up?"

André got up and went across to the chest of drawers beside the book-case at the back of his studio. He opened a

drawer, pulled out three pictures and brought them over to
me. He pointed out some of the more ridiculous mistakes
made by the forger which were still taking in some collectors. The first picture was on a wooden panel and appeared
to be the type of subject on a religious basis produced by
one or other of the early German masters of the fifteenth
century. He turned it over and I could see that it was made
up of several pieces of timber, all worm-eaten. André
exhorted me to look more carefully and closely. Then I
noticed that the worm-holes stopped suddenly where a cross
member had been inserted and then reappeared the other
side.

Pointing to what I had just observed, André said:

"Worm-holes in wood, unfortunately, all too often seem
to mesmerize the unwary, or perhaps better to say unthink-
ing; these people appear to take for granted that the
presence of holes made by the worm means age and that the
work is genuine. But it is a very simple matter for a forger
to obtain a piece of worm-eaten wood."

The second example André produced he handed me and
asked me to be careful and examine it very minutely too. As
far as I could see, it was a charming little landscape,
somewhat in the manner of the Venetian painter Guardi.
There was a small lake, little boats, and in the foreground
one could pick out a number of lively little figures such as
Guardi was so expert in indicating by the merest touches
and flicks of paint. I turned it over. Then André pointed
out where it had been relined, which would not be
suspicious because a picture pertaining to be by Guardi
would almost certainly, if on canvas, have needed to have
been relined; therefore, the canvas on the back would
appear new and so would the stretchers. Trying to pick up
what was wrong, I looked again at the front, but it all
appeared very convincing. Then André, with a palette

knife, very gently lifted one corner of the picture away from the reline, enough for me to see the back of the original canvas, and this too was quite obviously twentieth century. He gave me a magnifying glass and I examined the edges of this top canvas and I could now see how it had been given an ageing. My friend explained to me that this could be done by a little charring and staining, the result of which would be that when the picture had been relined, as in this case using a glue mixture, it would give a very convincing appearance. I asked him what had made him pull up the canvas like that in the first place. He told me I hadn't really looked at the picture closely enough. He pointed out that on the lake the little boats were certainly not of the time of Guardi; they had all the appearance of being late nineteenth century; and more than this a small building beside the lake was architecturally wrong for the supposed time. He explained that this business of getting things out of period was a common mistake with the not very bright forger. And that marine pictures often, if forged, held unintentional mistakes. "I have come across competently painted compositions with horrific faults in the rigging and with the wind apparently blowing the sails and flags in different directions," André told me.

He continued:

"On the other hand, it can also be that quite obviously by naïve measures the forger has set out to trap a buyer by such means as, say, the addition of an American flag to a craft that probably never went near the place or by adding a topographical background to suit the taste of the client."

The third example André showed me was again on canvas and appeared to be a beautiful flower-piece that might have been painted by Jan van Huysum or one of the other Dutch masters of this subject. It had all the lovely extravagance beloved of these painters, and the conceits of drops of water and small insects, with a caterpillar or two clambering over the leaves and petals. He told me that this was an odd one. Some years ago before the war he had been asked by an acquaintance if he would give an opinion on this picture, as it was thought that the painting could be completely genuine. André told me that at the time he had examined it very carefully but although he couldn't at once put his finger on it, it had worried him; the impasto, the little ridges of paint, had seemed just a little too heavy for a Dutch painter of the period it seemed to belong to. It had been recently relined, but it would have been difficult for him to ask if he could pick up a corner of the painting – the man would not have been very happy about it. Then André had looked again at those ridges of paint and he felt sure they were wrong. Eventually he had asked the man if he might very gently feel one of them with a needle in a part that was not important to the picture. The man had been a little put out by this but after a little thought had acquiesced. With a needle, André had found that the paint in the heart of these ridges was still moist and soft. Well, as André said, oil paints can take – if they are thick – up to ten or twenty years to really harden out, but certainly not two or three hundred. I asked André what had happened. He said he had explained to the man why the picture could not be right, and then the man had informed André that he had, a year or two previous, taken such a picture for restoration to someone who had kept it for a very long time indeed. Whatever the story behind the picture really was which André didn't himself know, the man had seemed so disgusted about his picture that he had told André to keep it, he didn't want it back. André could do what he liked with it, and André had kept it as an example, as he had just shown me.

André went on to outline the field of the forger, illustrating where he could with other examples. There are many pitfalls for the collector and there can be very large sums of money involved. It is quite possible, André told me, that you may come across a picture which will be backed by a seemingly faultless gilt-edged provenance. The forger, if he sets his mind to it, can be a master of a parcel of tricks not only in the finding and preparation of materials, but also in the simulation of the 'hand-writing' of a painter's strokes. Paint can be cracked by rolling or, in the case of a panel, by pounding with a hammer wrapped in a piece of soft material. When all the wiles have been deployed the result can often get by for a long time.

"I suppose," said André, "at the back of every gallery director's or collector's mind there must always be that shadowy figure who can murmur 'the perfect forgery is the one that is still undiscovered'. No one can give a hundred per cent comforting answer on that one."

"You must remember too, Edward," André had warned me, "there is a trick that fakers like to exploit. This is to produce a forgery and then to give it a fair working over and damage it quite thoroughly, after which they proceed to 'restore' it. A 'mystique' is then built up; for in some people's minds lurks a firm belief that a work which has been restored must be genuine."

Pundits are always appearing who go into the reasons for forging. Personally, as far as I am concerned, there may be the odd off-beat ones like Van Meergeren who have lumps of wood on their shoulders, but as the years have passed I have decided that most of these crafty-fingered gents are in it for the same reason I seem to be in it.

I suppose there is probably little doubt that there are few collections, national or private which are without the proverbial rotten apple in the barrel. It won't, of course, be only paintings; it can be sculpture, furniture, ceramics, silver; right across the board of art objects. The willing lads in the fake workshops are good marketeers; when they see a demand, why should they hang back if they can answer it? Not often enough, from the collector's point of view, do the brave ones open up and pull down the trappings of gaudy glamour. I had related to me not very long ago how one of the most erudite figures in the art world had come out quite clearly and said that the celebrated Lorenzo dei Medici in the National Gallery in Washington was an obvious forgery. And even as I am writing these memoirs I have heard whisperings in the undergrowth, which have come from scholarly lips, that the White House's most respected painting, the nation's official portrait of George Washington, which is attributed to Gilbert Stuart, is a fake.

But now to return for a moment to this matter of trying to detect deceitful and clever practices woven into the web of the forger. If one can fall back on ultra-violet rays, infra-red or even more sophisticated equipment some of the ploys can be exposed. For instance, an ultra-violet ray lamp will, in most cases, show up quite clearly if there have been recent additions.

I myself have come across a number of fakes, but fortunately, and quite a large proportion of my thanks goes to André, I haven't burnt my fingers too badly with them. Undoubtedly, as he told me, the longer the eye rests on the forgery, the more with experience it seems to die. It would be difficult for the man in the street, I think, to see the original of the 'Supper at Emmaus' by Van Meegeren, but, having seen it, one wonders how it ever took in those it did. But then, of course, this could be to an unknown degree because it had already been exposed as fraudulent. Observing the 'Emmaus' today, one notes various flaws; such as, there does not seem to be any bone in the left arm of the figure to the right of the front of the table. Amidst all the welter of rhetoric and praise that surrounded the launching of this canvas there seems to me to have been only one person who got through the junketing and that was one of Duveen's agents in Paris.

But, and it is a but, in the passionate excitement of a sale-room or the carefully rehearsed setting of a dealer's gallery, a forgery can take a lot of seeing. The situation is not helped in some cases by the very careful and all-encompassing wording of the catalogues that disclaim all responsibility on the part of the firms and sellers for any statements that appear regarding the genuineness, age, dates, provenances, origin, attribution. These they clearly say are only opinions and as such should not be relied upon. Ho hum! They do go on to say, however, if a buyer does find out that he has bought an outright fake within a limited number of days and if within another limited number of days he returns same, he will get his money back.

1946 went into 1947 and 1947 into 1948 and my visits continued to André. It was always I who went to him, as since the war he had not cared to travel. Anyway all his accessories were there with him in Belgium. I became closer and closer to him and I found I was having some twinges of conscience about what I was preparing myself for and felt pretty well ready to take on. There was something more about André than just sincerity, that was too small a word. Yes, after all these visits to him I felt paintings could never be quite the same thing to me again.

Here I was finding myself being torn between two duelling ecstasies. On the one side the elation at the thought of taking, and on the other, because of André, a growing respect — and call it perhaps love — for painters; men like Titian, the master who draped luminous glazes over his pictures to bring into being translucent richness;

the passionate flowing strokes of Rubens, possible, according to some, only because of a secret medium he had made that has since defied analysis; and then the one perhaps most of all, Rembrandt, with his handling of the mysteries of light and shade, particularly in those of his pictures that came late in his life. He had fallen from fashion in his last years, but who knows whether or not in those last compositions he was sharing some secret with a creative spirit outside our knowledge.

André had in his own way taken me as an apprentice and, true master that he was, had missed no step or detail that had been in his power to impart. A relationship had been struck which had an extraordinary intimacy. The depths of my feelings can therefore be imagined when on my return from rather prolonged visits to Spain and France, during the late autumn of 1949 I again made my way to see André only to find that in my rather longer than usual absence he had moved. As I stood waiting after having rung his bell several times with growing foreboding when I heard no footsteps hurrying across the floor and down the stairs, Berthe suddenly came running from her little house. She must have somehow spotted me or felt me there:

"Monsieur, you have not heard . . . our friend, Monsieur André – he is dead."

She too must have known something of André's worth, for she was obviously moved. She waited for a few seconds to compose herself, and then said:

"Could you perhaps come over to my house? As M. André was packing up to go to his cousin's after he had been taken ill the first time, he brought over to me a case and he said: "One day – I don't know when it will be – my friend, you know, he will return. Please give him this.""

I thanked her and took the case and put it in the car and

did not open it until I was back in the flat in London. Inside there were four panels of André's own paintings which he knew that I had always liked, and the rest was a large collection of note-books. When I opened one or two of them I saw that they were his studio-books, in which had been kept, almost with the regularity of a diary, all his experiences, findings and thoughts over a lifetime. As I replaced the contents of the case and was about to close the lid, I noticed that there was an envelope stuck on the inside with just the word 'Edward' in ink. Inside was a simple letter from a friend bidding goodbye, a friend with a feeling of presentiment that he would not be seeing me again.

Perhaps if André had lived a few years longer, things could have changed considerably and I would not now be writing this account.

Part Three

It was May 1950 and I was trundling across the northern plains of France towards Paris. The night before I had come over on the boat which connected with the train from Victoria.

What was I doing – I was not quite sure. I felt rather like a debutante who had mislaid her escort on her way to the 'coming out' ball.

For a long time after André had gone I had mooned about the flat and London; visiting galleries, meeting dealers, going to sales; moving in some sort of strange limbo and indulging in a state of funk. The romance of Mr Hood and his possible deeds, and the glamour I had envisaged seemed at the approach of reality to have left me. I had spent hours late at night and lying in bed, arguing the case to and fro between myself and my conscience. I had even gone so far as to buy copies of *The Times Educational Supplement* and other publications that listed possible positions for an art historian. I had made some tentative enquiries to various directors of galleries, headmasters, and university authorities. I think perhaps the responses that came from these, with their half-hearted enthusiasm at the thought of employing an inexperienced ex-lieutenant colonel, albeit art historian, lit up the fires that glowed in the promise of what I had earlier worked on.

I had dug out quite a bit more of the goings on of the handling and selling of art. Again I was not finding myself horrified by the comparison of how Mr Hood would work and how some of these merchants were working.

By nature I suppose I am someone who needs excitement. Like many thousands of others who had had a training in this subject for some six years of war, I was finding peace-time routine a trifle bland. It seemed that most of the good jobs or possibilities of good jobs had been held by those in reserved categories and were now blocked off. I had decided that it was time to have a go.

In my make-up there are many of the qualities of a chameleon. All my life I have found that I have been able to switch my personality, my style, manner of conversation, even perhaps my pattern of movements. I realized that all this could now be called to a good use. Disguise as such always seems to me to be strictly for the characters of fictional skulduggery. For not only is it a lot of bother to carry round a first-class actor's set of grease-paints, false hair, etcetera, but it also strikes me as a risky business. Thinking back, I had remembered several instances of when I had met people and then met them again when perhaps I was in a different mood, and I had noticed the second time it seemed they were not quite sure whether or not it was I.

On this business I had decided too that I was going to travel strictly alone. There were millions of people, thousands of places and hundreds of centres to make my little game possible and to stretch the law of coincidence. There was, however, one thing I promised myself. Come what may, if I fell under the feet of the law, I was most certainly going to be one of those characters who comes out with his hands up. The Mauser was out and the head was in.

During the last week after I had decided to go ahead I realized that a hideout on an island was not the best place. Road frontiers on a continent are one thing; boat-crossings and airports are quite another. It became clear that very shortly, if I was going to start operations, the flat must go. I must find some inconspicuous little place which I could run to like a fox to his earth. I had thought about Scandinavia – no, too far off the centre of things. Germany was obviously out, certainly for the moment. Italy was a possible. Belgium and Holland too small. France was big. France had then and still has marvellous little villages and towns scattered away south of Paris in that vast terrain that lies between that city and the Riviera; this could offer what I was after.

The transition from the coffee after my dinner on the train to the coast from Victoria the previous night to the fresh strong full-flavoured cup in the French dining-car worked an alchemy in me. Back flushed all the feelings that had roved around inside my mind prior to my extra-mural studies with André. The croissant was warm and crisp, the buzz of the French tongue around me gave me a sort of insular excitement, and by the time the train had drawn into the Gare du Nord it was definitely Mr Hood on his way.

I got down out of the carriage, caught the eye of a porter and joined in the rush. A taxi was found which took me to the hotel which I had booked three or four days before. After I had sorted my luggage and unpacked as much as I needed, I walked out into the eleven-o'clock air of Paris; a stirring amalgam of the smoke from the Gauloises, a whisper of perfume, something to do with fresh bread, and again, coffee. I threaded my way, window-shopping, through to the Champs-Elysées, where at the very first of the bars offering a table on the pavement I stopped for an aperitif. I bought a paper and browsed through the columns. I can recall that at the time I didn't really seem to have a plan firmly in my mind; yet somewhere in my head were very faint whisperings. Well, follow the breeze.

My eye caught in the 'what's going on section' that it was the opening day for the Salon — to give it its full title, that year was the hundred and sixty-third Exposition Officielle des Beaux-Arts — in the Grand Palais. That could be for me. I moved from the bar to a restaurant about fifty yards away. As something seemed to tell me that this was a sort of launch day, I did have a slight indulgence. By three o'clock I had paid the bill and wandered along to the Palais. This display of painting, architectural designs, decorative arts, prints and sculpture, if only by size tends to put the Royal Academy somewhat in the shade.

I wandered through the show in my usual way, waiting for something to really register. At somewhere past the halfway mark I found myself brought up by a landscape. Quite what it was that stopped me I am not sure, perhaps it was the painter's use of colours, or the way in which he had evoked the atmosphere in his scene. I felt a tap on the shoulder.

"Monsieur, you admire this painting?"

I turned and found myself being addressed by a dark swarthy individual in a light mauve-grey suit, a very expensive cream silk shirt and a dark wine full bow-tie.

"You are the artist?" I said.

"Oh no, no. Errrmm — I am the agent for the painter. He has been with my gallery for a number of years and he will be famous. Already his pictures are bringing good prices."

I explained to him that I was just visiting Paris; yes, I was very interested in paintings; I loved to see them, to admire them, and sometimes perhaps to buy them. He then courteously persuaded me to accompany him to a nearby café, thinking perhaps that with a little pressure he could make me take a deeper interest in his protégé.

He did make me take a deeper interest; not in his artist, however, but in himself. In his eagerness to impress he talked freely; in fact, after the third glass he let out that his main concern was, as he put it, in being a collector for profit. Like with some others I have come across, vanity, at times, can erase wisdom. When he thought he had found out how my own seeming interests lay, he suggested that I should join him for dinner at his house, which was some way out of Paris. He motioned me to the front passenger-seat of one of those large ballooned-out black American cars, which I noticed was quite new, and drove through the thickening traffic as the denizens from the offices broke up for the night and sped home. His principle was the same as that of many a taxi-driver; lean on the horn and you'll get through. He succeeded better than most because of the size of the vehicle and the loudness of the horn.

I had put him down as being single like myself. On the way out he conveniently filled in the details for me. He had thought of marriage many times but when satiated had withdrawn. During the war he had rather roughed it, according to him, in a small house in Spain — I couldn't help wondering what 'roughing it' meant for him. Immediately after the war he had had, again as he put it, a tremendous struggle to break in to the Paris art field. When we arrived at his house I was to realize just how successful he had been.

The small estate was set back some distance from the road, with the nearest neighbour I would estimate at least two hundred yards in any direction. The house itself could be termed school of le Corbusier; both outside and inside its appearance was unremarkable. It was what he had inside that raised the temperature in me. Not only was there a fine selection of furniture, rugs, cabinets of ceramics, cabinets of silver and objets d'art, but it was what was on the walls that really set me off.

In the main room, which looked out through large expanses of glass on to an expensively laid-out garden, hung what I supposed he might have called his stock. The Impressionists and their followers were well represented, so were the Realists of the French School, and I noted with interest a number of the foremost names from the East Anglian School. Interspersed with all these were a few examples from the main-stream movements of this century, Les Fauves, Dadaists, Surrealists, Cubists and Abstract.

He must have misread my enthusiasm because proudly he sailed through this room and three more on the ground-floor and also up the stairs to a spacious landing. He pointed out each painting as we came to it and recited the provenance; which in some cases was unusual to put it mildly. I asked one or two innocent questions and the replies were enlightening; mostly so when he discussed openly how he had come by some specimens. A number of these methods were nothing more nor less than 'knocking'. Other instances pointed to the fact that he probably had an undertaker as an informant and he was very likely working fist-in-hand with a twisted solicitor.

After dinner had been served, his one and only servant, as he had informed me, a somewhat ageing lady who could have been of Corsican origin, brought the coffee and liqueurs into the large lounge and in a gruff grumble said if that was all, she'd be going.

As he drove me back to my hotel he chattered away inconsequentially. He asked me if I was in Paris for long. I told him that I wasn't sure how many days I would be staying. He remarked that there was an exciting party at a château not too far from the city in three days' time and there would be some interesting people there for me to meet, and he would like to take me with him. I said that it might be that I would have left by then. But he gave me his phone number and said to ring him if it would be possible. The party would be starting at nine and would be going on into the early hours, finishing somewhere around two or three.

The next morning, bearing in mind what my host of the night before had told me about the forthcoming party, I went down to reception and told them that I would have to cut short my stay and must leave that day. I packed, paid my bill, and managed to hire a car from close-by for three days. I decided I could usefully spend my time in a preliminary 'recce' for the little house I was seeking. Leaving Paris, I drove away to the south and headed towards Orleans, Gien and Bourges. I arrived about tea-time in a likely looking area, fixed myself up at a small auberge and drove around until the light had gone. All the next day I kept up the search and by late evening had a promising short list of possible districts.

The following midday I drove back to Paris and arrived in the area of my new acquaintance's house just as the dusk was deepening. I drew the car off the main road into a small secluded wooded lane and whiled away my patience until eleven o'clock when I judged the Corsican house-lady and also her employer would long ago have left.

I restarted the car and drove past the entrance to his drive and parked in between a high brick wall and deserted sheds in a turning off to the right. Leaving the car, I soft-footed back towards his drive. Before I got there I found an easy entrance to his mini-estate; and helped by the light of a half-moon I climbed over a low stone wall and through a loosely planted hedge.

Up to now I don't think that I had really hoisted in that

this was going to be any different from the time that I did over Ernst's place. But as I approached the house I did have to pause and gather up the entrails, because it *was* different. Mr Hood was about to break the law for the first time.

I went right round the house; all the windows were tight-shut; there was no sign of a light anywhere. I tried the front door first, after having pulled on a pair of gloves and feeling strangely professional by so doing. The handle turned but it held firm on the latch-lock I could just make out below eye-level. Windows were next, but again no luck; they were not only shut but latched. Gradually, working my way round, I came to the back-door. I tried the handle and it opened with only the slightest creak. Bless the Corsican, she must have had what might be called later a slip of the memory.

On the night of the dinner with my host I had selected the most suitable piece from his stock for what was to be my act of initiation. This was a pastel of a dancer by Degas. Not only was this drawing quite small, but it had been framed with a narrow mount and with the frame was not more than about sixteen by fourteen inches. It would also realize a fair price.

The Degas hung just to the right of the door behind his desk in the study. I did cautiously shine the light of a small torch behind the frame to see if there were any untoward surprises, but there were none. The wire could just be flicked off the hook and the picture was free.

For a few moments after this seemingly ridiculous victory I stood motionless but there was hardly a sound. A dull mumble of traffic from the distant road came through and there was a slight swishing of the breezes through a row of cupressus outside the windows; apart from these there was the thump-bumping of my heart.

To confuse matters a bit I went back to the kitchen and locked the back-door and then went out through the front door, giving it just enough of a slam to push the latch home. So more than probable the Corsican's slip would not be picked up, and means of entry would remain a mystery.

I was back in the car and snugly ensconced in yet another small auberge a few minutes before midnight.

The following day I returned the car and travelled back to England by the same route that I had come. The Degas I had packed away at the bottom of the larger of my two cases. This action proved a crass piece of stupidity, forgetfulness, pride, call it what you like; because when I arrived at Dover the Customs official asked me if I had anything to declare and then in the same breath demanded that I open the big case. I tried to appear completely unmoved so as not to show the visions of Wormwood Scrubs, Parkhurst, and the rest which were flickering behind my eyes. He lifted a corner of my dressing-gown with one hand and burrowed down with the other past pyjamas, socks, handkerchiefs. He must have sensed something hard. He pulled out the torch, smiled wryly, and replaced it. He then ran a hand along the other end of the case and I can only imagine must have been within a hairbreadth of the picture at the bottom. He closed the case, smiled at me, put on the requisite chalk mark, and I was through. More than shaken, I walked rather stilt-legged away to find some liquid solace until I boarded the train for London.

For the next week I don't think that anybody else in London studied so assiduously every French newspaper that came to hand as I did. But there was not the smallest mention of my particular exploit.

I did not know at the time a possible explanation for this. It was only much later on when I really began to burrow into the stranger aspects of art crimes that some reasons came up. Apparently a surprising number of collectors never report thefts from their collections at all. It may be their vanity precludes them from doing this; in that, they don't want to advertise the fact that their treasures can be so easily fiddled away. It may be from some rather twisted idea about protection; that if they have some objects stolen the ensuing publicity will draw the further attentions of the light-fingered fraternity, which of course at times it certainly does. Gradually though, another reason came to my knowledge. This was that some collectors couldn't very well report the thefts because of the simple fact that many of the objects they had in their collections might have been procured in various shadowy ways. It made it much easier for me.

The lease on the flat in London had another two months to run and when the agent asked me if I wanted a further span, at of course an increased rent, I told him that I would be giving it up. During this time I let the little pastel dancer rest. It wasn't until there was just a fortnight to go that I sallied forth to exchange her for the ready. The character I had selected went through all the usual pantomime and then eventually came up with a figure which represented about one sixth of the value; but, even so, this was comfortably into four figures and, better still, as with these things, it was handed over in good folding money, albeit in mixed currencies, pounds, dollars, Swiss francs, but all easily convertible. It was becoming clearer to me that London was not the best place to trade in. Easy enough perhaps to get a reasonable drop for the stuff up to around £5,000 but after that not on.

Like a good gun-dog I kept my nose to the ground and, with a word from here and a hint from there, the scene slowly began to show itself and somewhat cautiously let me in.

The day after I had sold the Degas I had had a letter from the house-agent with whom I had left my needs in France. He sent me details of four likely looking places. This was handy, as I was wondering where I was going to hole-up when the flat had gone. Without more ado, I got the garage to give the faithful old Minx the once-over. I managed to get a booking on a boat and within just forty-eight hours I was in the area having a look-see at the properties.

The first two were quite useless, but the third one, which was on the outskirts of a small town, I very soon found had just what was needed. It was compact and stone built, with deep orange-red tiles. On the ground-floor it had a living-room, kitchen and scullery. In the latter, tucked away in a corner was a kind of white glazed earthenware bath about two feet square and a foot deep with a ramshackle shower over the top. The water appeared to be heated either by the antique range in the kitchen or an equally ancient contraption that used two wicks that I imagined must burn paraffin. Upstairs there were two reasonably sized bedrooms; one I ear-marked as a study; there was also a small box-room about four feet by seven. The house stood alone in a tiny garden which sported an old apple tree, two or three shrubs and what looked like a vine draped over a rough back-porch. On one side was a lofty concrete-block grain store, not exactly pretty; on the other side was a short terrace of sturdy villas with all their windows looking demurely at the street. In the front the garden was separated from the road by a low stone wall surmounted by iron railings some six feet high and an iron gate to match. At the back there was a high rubble wall capped with brick reaching up to about eleven feet.

The price the owner was asking, through the agent, was reasonable. Said owner, I gathered, had departed to the sunnier climes of Egypt. After a brief haggle, which did bring it down slightly, the agent and I came to an agreement. With what I had on me I was able to give him half the figure there and then in dollars, and told him that I would arrange for a bank draft to be sent immediately. We parted in good humour and he handed me the receipt and said I might as well have the plans and a little map, and that the deeds and other documents would be sent from the solicitor.

I went once more back into the house just to take some measurements, as I hoped that the furniture and carpets I had in London could be fitted in satisfactorily.

A drive to Calais, a crossing, and I was back in the flat, whereupon I knew I had to get busy right away. I had already tentatively spoken to a small remover with a light van, which was all that would be needed for what I had. I asked him how soon he could make the trip. I found that it was actually four days after the lease was up. But he was agreeable to loading the furniture and the bits and pieces before that date.

There was, of course, the matter of my investments, but owing to currency restrictions, etcetera, at this time I could see little else to do with them than to leave them as they were. The income could accrue, for I was sure I should be nipping back now and then. I drew out the surplus cash in my current and deposit accounts, having given notice as regards the latter earlier. As the rather amazed and, I could sense, questioning clerk handed over just on two thousand six hundred, I murmured something about going on a holiday to Scotland to look round for some antiques.

I found when packing that during my studies I had accumulated a fair old tonnage in books, and after spending about an hour running through them I discovered I had just over one hundred titles that had already served their purpose and which I felt I wouldn't need again. There was no point in humping these along too, so I packed them up in four large cartons and took them down to the Minx. I recalled the name of a second-hand bookseller in Kent whom my father used to deal with. I thought there might be an off-chance that he was still around. With the help of telephone enquiries I did find his number and, what was more, in a couple of minutes was speaking to him. I arranged to go down that afternoon.

It was fine and the idea of a run down to Kent was attractive. It was one of those early autumn pleasures; leaves were beginning to exchange greens for russets, golds and deep browns. The glimpses I got of the countryside, and the Medway, as it writhed past Tonbridge, brought on an attack of nostalgia and a little bit of sadness that I was, to a degree, voluntarily exiling myself.

The bookseller, when I found him, was charming and began by asking all about what had happened over my father and mother, and was openly distressed when he learnt what had occurred. This meeting with him and our talk tugged again at the emotional side. When I left I could not help but feel that that kind man had actually given me much more than he should have done for the books.

I started to drive back and found as I was entering Tonbridge that it was coming up to seven o'clock, and feeling a pang of hunger, I parked the car and walked in to the Rose and Crown for a couple of gins and what turned out to be a good *table d'hôte* dinner.

The meal over, I was on my way again by nine. The main road with its heavy traffic didn't hold much attraction, so I swung off into the side roads and lanes that tangled away between Tonbridge, Edenbridge, Westerham and Sevenoaks. About half an hour after I had left I was driving along a fairly lonely stretch only sparsely built-up. I passed

one opulent large house on the right where they were
obviously in the throes of a fruity party. Cars and
chauffeurs filled the drive. Doors were open and there were
sounds of much merry-making.

I don't know what made me stop but something must
have breathed into an ear. I drew off the road about a
quarter of a mile past the house, put out the lights, locked
the car up, and walked back towards the building through a
convenient plantation of mixed trees which in the approaching darkness gave me complete cover. I managed to work
my way round behind the house and approached nearer to it
through a thick shrubbery. This in its turn finally landed
me so that I was hidden in a large rhododendron bush a
bare ten yards from the side of the house. I now had an
excellent view of what was happening not only at the side,
but also in the front. Set in the side wall was a wide
double-doored French window which gave me a clear sight
of the interior of their main reception room. Everything
was brightly lit, and the guests and hosts seemed well on
the way to an alcoholic haze.

I was so close that I was able to examine the room
carefully. What struck my eye at once was what appeared to
be an excellent example of the Dutch seventeenth-century
Marine School. Could it be, I wondered, by one of the Van
de Valdes, either Willem the Younger or Willem the
Elder? The acquisitive urge took me very strongly and I
felt I just had to have it. This idea, however, seemed rather
idiotic, because – how?

But the answer was soon to present itself; for within what
must have been about ten minutes after my arrival in the
midst of the rhododendrons the party began to break up,
and swiftly. By what I could hear they were all going on to
one of the guests' houses, including the hosts, and to my
astonishment, the hosts were volunteering that their two

servants should go along as well to help serve what was apparently to be a large buffet supper, and which the two servants could then help to clear up. Soon cars began to move piled with slightly, or more than slightly, inebriated guests. There were spurts of gravel as they departed down the drive, and within about another ten minutes every light in the house had gone out, the front door had been slammed, and every one had left, except the watching figure in the rhododendron bush, who by now was in a slight trance, brought on by a stroke of unexpected good fortune. I still hadn't learnt to control this cataleptic condition which descended upon me at such times, and I was becoming aware that it could lead to difficulties. What had caused it this time was, that our orgy-bent hosts had slammed the front door – yes, but had totally forgotten about the wide-open French windows.

By now it was almost completely dark but there was just enough of that back reflection from a departed sun to allow me to avoid tripping over the rockery or tripping up on the steps; also I could still make out a way across the room to the painting. I gave a cursory glance behind the frame with the help of my torch for any snags. There were none. I lifted the painting off the wall and I was out of the French windows and back in the Minx in six minutes flat I reckon, and once more purring along towards London.

When I got back to the flat I surveyed my prize and was delighted to see that it was by Willem the Younger, who had been born in 1633 and lived until about 1707. The title of my acquisition was 'Dutch Fleet in a Calm'. It measured $21\frac{1}{2}$ by $19\frac{1}{4}$ inches. This painter at his best has a quality which I find attractive. He handles the light on the water in a superb way, and the whole placing of his vessels, as well as the details of the rigging and the sails are carried out most convincingly. My next thought was, how was I going to get this treasure out of the country? I recalled quite clearly my *gaffe* when bringing in the Degas, and this I was not going to repeat. I thought about it for sometime, and then decided that one way which would be possible would be to cut the canvas from its stretcher and disguise it, rather in the manner of a sandwich, with a larger canvas.

The next morning I went off to a local art dealer and bought three yards of ready-primed canvas, a twenty-five by thirty-inch stretcher, a light sketching-easel, some oil painting materials, and a small card folio large enough for the 'Dutch Fleet'. I took this lot back to the flat. Whereupon I first laid out the canvas and cut it up into three pieces large enough to fit the twenty-five by thirty-inch stretcher. The first piece I trimmed exactly to the stretcher size and stapled it on to the stretcher. Then into the centre of the second piece I cut out a hole $21\frac{1}{2}$ by $19\frac{1}{4}$ inches which would fit the Van de Velde. I also trimmed this second piece exactly to fit the stretcher and stapled it into position on top of the first piece. Next I cut the Van de Velde from its stretcher, and following this I put some small spots of water-soluble glue on the corners at the back of the Van de Velde and placed it face up into position in the hole in the second canvas.

When the glue had set I then took the third piece of canvas and laid it over the top of the previous two and the painting and tacked it down in the normal way to the sides and back of the stretcher. Finally, a few taps on the wedges in the corners of the stretcher made the whole thing tight, and as far as I could see well disguised.

The weight differential was minimal. Who was going to suspect an innocent canvas which an artist was apparently taking with him on a painting holiday was a missing Van de Velde, even if and when it got out about one being missing? The sizes were totally different. This turned out to be a device I was to use a number of times in the following years. The main trick about it, apart from the canvas stretching, was to make sure that the picture being so transported fitted exactly into the mount hole, so that there would be no ridge or dent-line to be seen or felt. It was only later on when the Customs hotted things up that I decided it was wise to cease this practice.

My friend with his removal van duly arrived and in a matter of a couple of hours had packed up the load and I was left with just one small suit-case of clothes to last me for a few days, and my artist's equipment: the canvas, which had now been clipped to the front of the easel with the folio behind it, and the tubes of paint, brushes, suitably dirtied palette, and some bottles of turpentine and linseed oil, all done up in an old canvas bag with a shoulder strap. It was altogether an innocent and impressive outfit.

One last matter, the Minx had to go to the garage to be sold. I had a distasteful argument, but emerged not too badly down on the deal, and made for the station for the first part of the journey to France.

The night-boat and train the other end landed me in Paris at a convenient hour in the morning. First I got a taxi to take me to the nearest big Renault dealer. There, after a bit of sniffing around, I got myself not exactly a bargain, but a convenient car which had not been too badly hammered, and which had only 18,000 kilometres on the clock. I settled the bill for this, gathered up the necessary papers, and then drove out of Paris a little way into the country, until I could find a reasonably deserted stopping place.

Thereupon, with a tack lifter and a pair of plyers I took the top canvas off the stretcher and very gently, using a palette knife, broke the little glue spots and lifted the Van de Velde clear. It seemed to have survived its slightly unorthodox method of travel very well. I opened the cardboard folio and placed the painting inside and put it on the right-hand side front seat. After this, I took off the other two pieces of canvas, folded them up, dismantled the stretcher, and put the lot in the boot.

How I wished that André was still around because he was just the person I needed to prepare the painting for selling. But there was a restorer in Paris that I remembered making a note of in one of my sessions with André. Driving back towards the city, I stopped at a call-box and gave this man a ring and found with relief that he was still operating. I then drove along to his studio which was in Montmartre. He examined the picture and suggested that it would be best first to take off an earlier reline that was of rather poor thin weak canvas and then do the job properly on a more substantial material. We had a little discussion about the method he would use. He also pointed out that there were one or two small scratches in the varnish, but he was sure these were only in the varnish and that the paint film was not affected at all. He said that he would have the work done within a month.

I now journeyed on from Paris down to the south and the hideaway. My removal friend was not due to arrive until the next day and I spent my time doing a little charring around the house. Actually it had been left well scoured and did not need much more than a good go through with a broom and duster.

Punctually on time the van arrived and the driver kindly helped me lay the odd carpet and fiddle the furniture around to suit my taste. At the end, although it was a little sparse, it was quite livable in for the moment. I offered to bed him down for the night, but he gave a lurid cockney wink and told me that he thought he would be having a look at the lights of Paris, and he was gone.

Some three weeks later I gave the restorer a ring to

enquire about progress and found that the picture would be ready for me in three days time. After this interval I drove up to Paris to collect it. He had done an excellent job; the reline was perfect, and where the scratches had been there was now no sign of damage at all. What he had done, he told me, was to remove the old varnish, as it was slightly yellowed from age, and to renew it.

I felt in a slight dilemma with regard to the disposal. I wasn't sure how much hullabaloo had been raised back in England or even for that matter if there had been much inquiry at all. But although Holland, with Amsterdam and Rotterdam, seemed to be a good place, it also had a warning red-light, that if some investigation had been going on it would be likely that a description and the size of the painting would have been circulated there. After some thought, I decided to visit the Alsace character and see how I would fare. Strangely enough, this time he seemed more amenable. He went into raptures, as far as it was possible for him to do so, over the 'Dutch Fleet in a Calm'. What was more, within a few minutes he made me a very reasonable offer indeed and accepted with good grace when I gently pushed it up to the next round figure. As before he paid from what appeared to be an inexhaustible supply of dollars. The funding was coming along, slowly, but quite nicely.

*　　*　　*

It was now some two years later, early September, 1952. I am a little ashamed to say that during these two years I had not been exactly active. The fact that there is a comfortable amount available in a bank or banks tends to lull me into a state of languor. I suppose there is a chunk of that chameleon which responds to this and can over-rule the excitement seeker who lives with it. Maybe I wasn't exactly in the Cadillac or Rolls class yet. But these outback places in France exert an atmosphere that can grind to a slow trot the most vigorous galloper. Wine, lashings of gorgeous fruit and cheese. What more?

I think I have always had a penchant for old buildings, particularly churches, cathedrals and abbeys. There is something about the feeling that they have, and they alone. The sensation they engender for me is one which is compounded of admiration of the craftsmanship, the designing that has gone into them, and, in many cases, skills that are now lost. I can get a sense of peace too, but it is tinged with sadness that it is unlikely that the likes of these will ever be built again. From where I was living I was able to indulge myself with this love quite freely. As an amateur photographer, I had built up quite a collection of studies. I had even, in my rather lowly manner, filled a few sketch-books of details that had caught my eye.

On this day I had motored over to Bourges. The grapes were heavy on the vines and the landscape was dry and hot. Grass viewed from the distance across the hills was more the colour of golden brown sand than green.

Bourges was a place that I had visited several times already because the cathedral held a particular spell for me. The best approach I had found was to park the car and walk up the cobbled streets which lead to that quite amazing façade of the West front with the five porches. Although it is true this was defaced by the Huguenots, the strength and quality are still there. The porches are unusual in the way they are set on a platform reached by I seem to remember about sixteen stone steps.

The carving with which the early craftsmen enriched the surfaces of some early Gothic buildings reads to me like a story-book. Here, at Bourges, I had found I could spend the best part of an hour in front of these five porches, looking with wonder at the work of those early masons who had gone beyond the working difficulties of carving the stone to produce a plethora of images which sometimes seemed almost like a strip-visual story. Over the centre porch with the double entrance are scenes from the Last Judgement. There stands the dignified St Michael, with figures either side of him, and particularly perhaps those below, which always remind me of those of Bosch or Pieter 'Hell' Breughel. Some of the carving is almost in the round; I was fascinated by its depth; and it is amazing how gently time has dealt with parts of it.

Inside the cathedral there is height; it is some hundred and twenty-five feet up to the vaulting. I had previously visited the crypt and knew there were traces of a ninth-century Carolingian building. Perhaps, I thought, this was the key to the attraction of many of these great places — their having stood for age on age on age.

I was standing gazing up yet again at the window of the Prodigal Son, which had been made about 1215 to 1220, and which had been given by the tanners of the city, when, quite out of the blue, a soft American voice spoke to me from behind:

"Excuse me, sir, may I break in?"

I turned; this was one of the standard approaches, and I wondered what next. The voice went on:

"I must take me a photo of what you're looking at. It's just great. I wonder if you'd be so good, sir, as to hold and steady my tripod for me?"

I replied: "Certainly," and looked around to see if any guardians of the cathedral were in evidence, as I wasn't quite sure if photography was allowed inside or not. I had restricted my own to outside. But this thought didn't seem to deter my new acquaintance. He was remarkably efficient with the handling of his camera, and I could only imagine he was used to taking pictures quickly in places where permission might be doubtful. After he had taken his shots and folded the tripod, he went on:

"I'm sure grateful to you, sir." Then there was a slight pause, and I could almost hear him inwardly begging me to give him a chance to prolong the conversation. What of it? The day had been pleasant. The afternoon was wearing on. I had nothing to do, and I felt amiable.

"That's a fine looking camera you've got there," I opened up.

"Oh, yes. It's done me well over the years. It's a Leica I got just before the war. The Germans could sure make cameras. Are you staying here, sir?"

"No, I'm just like yourself I expect, visiting, and admiring it."

"Oh, gee, the trouble is, where I come from, back in Virginia, there's nothing like this; and when one does come over here to Europe, one's got to take every chance one can."

The conversation trickled on as we sauntered round the cathedral together. Before coming out, we had to linger for a moment or two at the north door. My friend was really taken with the idea that it dated from as far back as 1160 and was a relic of an earlier Romanesque church. At this point, in a generous moment, I suggested that we go and have a drink. He obviously welcomed the idea, and together we walked across the open space on this side and turned down into the labyrinthine web of cobbled streets until we came to a reasonable looking bar. I asked him what he would have and rather surprisingly he didn't choose the standard Scotch on the rocks, but went for a dark vermouth. I shared his choice. When the waiter had set the glasses on the table the American went on:

"I'm just staying here for a few days. I'm on my way back from Finland, and I catch the boat from Southampton in about six weeks time. I'm trying to take in as much as I can before then. You might ask what I was doing up in Finland. Well, I'm a member of my sports club back in the States and I've just been up there to see the 15th Olympic Games. It was quite something. I must say your Lord Burghley gave a fine speech on the opening and it was great to see the old-timer Paavo Nurmi come tracking on to the stadium with the torch. Gee, but you should have seen that scatter-brained girl all decked up looking like some Greek goddess in white; she called herself the Angel of Peace and she was up there trying to make some speech on the rostrum. For a moment she had everybody fooled; even the President of Finland was there waving his hands together for her."

I broke in: "Did you watch all the games there, the whole time?"

"Well, I guess I was in my seat for every major event, especially the long distance runs; that's what really gets me, moves me. And to see the way Zatopek came rushing round in the last bit of that 10,000 metres . . . boy, do you know he knocked 42.6 seconds off his own record."

Then in the at times pleasantly surprising naïve way that some of his countrymen do, my new acquaintance went on:

"I must say I'm enjoying myself out here, but I'm just longing to get back to the States and my stables. You know, sir, out there I have a hobby breeding horses."

I could only mumble that I didn't know.

He rattled on about how his father had come over to America in the very early years of the century and had got into some part – I couldn't be quite sure what it was – of the automobile boom. He had made a packet which he had kindly passed on to my friend. Another drink later, and he told me his full name, but I shall call him Robert. He then turned to me and said:

"Oh, excuse me, I don't know your name." I told him what I felt would serve as a current alias and fed him the Christian name of Charles. Then, seeing that his eyes were flashing signals that he was about to ask what I did, I saved him the trouble by continuing:

"I'm a student of architecture and the arts generally, but perhaps especially of paintings, and I'm travelling round in France, partly enjoying myself and partly doing some work at the same time." His eyes lit up at this information.

"Gee, you're some kind of connoisseur."

"Well, I suppose you could put it like that."

"My goodness, Charles, I think that maybe you could do me a service."

"If you think I can."

"Well now, I'm, as I told you, running a stable, and I've got some great horses. I'm trying to make everything as authentic as I can back there. I've got me a big house behind some lovely paddocks." I understood him; in fact, what he was saying was turning up the burners under my ideas department.

He continued: "Well now, what I'm wondering is this. I don't know anybody over here. I've only been to Europe just once before, and that was not voluntary, if you understand me. I was over here with one of the divisions that was ploughing their way across into Germany. Now what I want is . . . I want paintings, pictures of animals . . . well really old English sporting pictures, of horses in particular because they'd look just grand in my house. You must be travelling round and meeting a lot of people."

I butted in here: "Well, I might be able to help you; in fact, I do, in a quiet way, go in for a little dealing for friends if I can find what they want."

He came again: "Of all the luck. Here. Who'd ever think I'd walk into this in Bourges. Charles, you've got to come and have some dinner with me. We are going to sort out some details."

We drained our glasses and he led the way down the street across two others and then into the Place Jacques Coeur where there is the restaurant of the same name, which had opened up just after the war. He must have been there before, perhaps it was for lunch or dinner the previous night; for the head waiter welcomed him and led us to a quiet table at one side.

The menu was not over large and from it I chose a Charentais melon, which when it came was nestled into a bed of crushed ice and was as delicious as all the rest of its brothers and sisters that I had had in the past few weeks. I followed it up with one of the specialities of the Jacques Coeur, rognons de veau berrichonne, which was as interesting and succulent as it sounded; and finished with a sweet that I can very seldom resist if it is on a menu, profiteroles au chocolat. My transatlantic friend proved to be a good host and he knew his wine; he wasn't diverted by the waiter's first suggestions, but picked out a delicious bottle of Reuilly. After the meal we sat back with a pot of fine coffee and two large glasses of eau de vie which had a faint tang of pears, and lit up dark aromatic cigars.

I was trying to analyse my friend. Was he genuine or could there be some kind of tangle coming up? On the other side of my mind, however, was the money-box rattling away. He certainly seemed to know what he wanted, because over the dinner and later he gave me a fair old briefing. He didn't want some of those old hack portraits. I forgave him his pun. He wanted something with a bit of character. He said:

"Course, what I'd really like is a Stubbs. But I guess there aren't all those many around." I agreed with him and listened whilst he went on:

"I've seen a painting a friend of mine's got who lives just outside New York. It's by somebody called Marshall. Now he's a painter. Boy! I'd like something by him. I tell you what, Charles, I'm like my dad, I'm plain speaking and plain wanting. How say, you look out four good paintings, not too big, mind you; pictures with something to them? 'Cause I got four places in my dining-room in which I could just hang them. You know what I want; you heard what I said during dinner. I want quality."

I thought I had better try and find out exactly how much my friend envisaged paying for this quality.

He went on, "Well, I guess I know what these things cost. I guess just to start with; say, don't go over a hundred thousand dollars."

I rather liked that 'to start with' bit.

"You give me the stuff with this, Charles, and who knows we may do business again. How long do you think it will take for you to chase these up?"

"Well . . . errr . . . you can't do it overnight. You say you are sailing from Southampton in six weeks' time. That's somewhere about past the middle of October. I should think I could have news for you say around the 2nd or 3rd of the month. Where can I contact you, Robert?"

He took out his diary. "Well, I'm spending the last fortnight of my trip in London; most in the city, but dodging out now and then. I'll be staying at the Piccadilly Hotel."

I made a note of this, and he said, "That's just fine en, Charles."

I went on, "Would you like me to lay on the packing and transport if I find what you are after?"

He looked up and gave a bit of a wink. "Oh no, Charles, I guess I got that side of things buttoned up. I've a friend who's on the board of one of these freight lines which runs out of New York and calls into Southampton and other places. I guess I can arrange the shipping. By the way, don't bother about no frames; they just waste space. I can easy check on a boat that'll be about the right time. I don't mind letting you know, but they've hiked a good few packing cases across the Atlantic for me. By the way, Charles, what I do want you to know is that I'm paying your expenses over and above for this." I tried to demur but fortunately he was completely firm; and who was I to argue! We parted on close terms, and I drove away a little dizzily after another glass of eau de vie.

Next morning I did sleep rather late, but after a good mug of black coffee I came awake and went into my study and unlocked the cupboard where I kept André's note-books and also several thick ones of my own. The latter I took out and thumbed through the index. These books I had been working on for several years; in fact, ever since I started with André and really began to get to grips with matters. These thick commonplace books, in short are a 'where is it, what is it, who painted it' on a fairly elaborate scale. Over the years, studying sales reports, going through old records, catalogues, newspaper cuttings and the rest, I had been building up a fairly comprehensive listing of where the cream of paintings could be found. The lists were primarily concerned with private residences, houses, castles, schlosses, châteaux and so on. Although perhaps slightly weighted in favour of Britain, they had even then a fairly good coverage of the Continent. Certainly Germany, Italy, France, Holland and Belgium were well represented. I had taken a lot of pains with these records and made a triple index which had literally taken me days to do, and which, of course, I have continued adding to. This index shows the places, the painters and the subjects. There are headings such as portraits, landscapes, still life, genre and sporting.

9—MOAAT * *

Other books show specimen signatures, paper watermarks, etcetera.

By the time I was finishing my third mug of coffee that morning I had an interesting list compiled. But most of these I could see, to put it mildly, would prove pretty fruity operations. Admittedly, they held what my friend was seeking. But I rather liked my life as it was at the moment in France and I wanted it to continue that way.

I was nearly at the bottom of the sporting section by now, when I came across a list of about thirty paintings which had been bought quite recently by one of those millionaires who had made his lump by wheeling around the supply lines of the hardware we had all been using not many years before. He lived hidden away in an off-track part of Hampshire. I did not know the house but I could recall once having been to the village. It was one of those miniature affairs with a couple of dozen houses, half a shop and a pub. I somehow thought that this could be the lad to investigate first.

If possible I always like to have a little enjoyment on such jaunts. So the next day, having made a reservation for the following one on the boat, I drove down into Switzerland just to see how matters were progressing in the numbered account. All seemed satisfactory and I felt I could draw out an appreciable sum for expenses. I spent the night in Dijon and made an early start for the boat next morning. After I had landed in Dover I decided to spend the night there. This was followed by a leisured breakfast and then I was off down to Hampshire, where I fixed myself up for a few days at a quiet inn near Alresford.

The following morning I motored in the direction of my millionaire's mansion. After about an hour's drive I found it comfortably placed between a quarter and half a mile from a small village. It was tucked into a sheltering hill with a clump of firs and evergreens set each side of it rather like half-drawn curtains. Through these could be glimpsed the main entrance under a form of bastardized Grecian portico, a few of the windows and a couple of rather elongated chimneys. What I did notice was that obviously the place was in the hands of the builders. There was a lorry outside, piles of bricks, slates, pipes and other gear.

It was while I was having a crust of bread and a wedge of cheese with a pint in the very friendly village local that three of the lads from the builder's gang came in, and with their talk to the landlord, in a very short time they had kindly put me in the know of what was going on.

They had a big job on at the big house. The roof had to come off; plumbing was being re-done; and the wiring too; and some stonework had to be repaired. They weren't working Saturdays or overtime, so it wasn't going to be finished before the beginning of December. I had a second pint to spin it out. A few minutes later I learnt that 'his nibs' had gone off to his Mediterranean villa until the work was finished. His man-servant had gone with him plus one of the maids with Mrs 'nibs', and the rest of the indoor staff had been given time off. The two gardeners were only working mornings. The housekeeper had been lodged in a near by boarding-house but she was coming in every morning to let them in and every evening to lock up after they had finished for the day. How observant was this housekeeper I wondered to myself. One of them had made a joke about her; apparently she wasn't very popular in the village. An interesting point I had gathered, as the conversation had continued, was that she had only joined the household about the middle of August, just a fortnight before the owner and his wife had gone off. I couldn't help wondering if he had made sufficiently sure that her references were reliable.

During that afternoon I studied the lay-out carefully. On the way back to my inn I stopped and bought a large-scale map of the area. In the evening I looked this over. I found that there was a convenient minor road which went up along the spine of the hill that was at the back of the house. I recalled from my viewing that I should be able to get a good look from up there.

The next morning I set off in the same direction. I found the small road after a little difficulty, as it was approached by a tangle of lefts and rights behind the village. Eventually I got on to it and climbed up through the woods and then found myself driving along the top of the hill, as I had guessed, but conveniently hidden by a fairly dense hedge of holly and beech. I parked the car and walked along until I judged myself opposite to the back of the house. Here once again fortune favoured me, because the hedge at this place thinned out and I was able to look down on my prey. I could see straight away that the house was built on a square plan with an open court-yard in the middle. What was more, my building 'friends' were hard at it, stripping the roof. To enable them to do this, they had not only a ladder up from the front of the house, but also one up from the internal court-yard. I could just make out that there appeared to be at least one door opening out of the house into the court-yard.

The day was Wednesday, so I had at least forty-eight hours to get through until I could go to work. When I returned to my inn I extended my stay until Saturday morning.

Friday afternoon found me once more on my way, and by about half past three I was again on top of the hill; but this time not so far along. I had parked the car in a small deserted quarry. I had loaded myself with the standard kit of gloves, torch, screwdriver, pliers and pocket-knife, and had wended my way down through the woods until I had found a hidden spot from which I could observe movements. The time was then about a quarter past four.

At a quarter to five a small Austin car drove up and a severe-looking woman with a tight bun, dark-rimmed glasses, undershot, and wearing a plain tailored dark grey suit got out and went into the house. The housekeeper I presumed. Shortly afterwards the labourers started to come down from the roof and out of different parts of the house. I noticed with comfort they made no attempt to move either of the long ladders. They got into their truck and drove away. A further ten minutes and the housekeeper came into sight once more. She turned and locked the front door and got back into her car and also left.

Yes, it looked as though I really would have to break in. Well, it was unlikely anybody in the village would hear the noise of broken glass, but the mess would advertise matters on the next Monday morning.

I was now stuck with a rather chilly wait until about ten o'clock when I judged it would be reasonable to start things moving.

There was a vague kind of thinness to the darkness from a weak half-moon, just enough to get a few guide-lines from. I drew on my gloves and walked across to the house; rather fruitlessly I thought, I went through the routine of trying the front door, the side-door and the back-door. The windows were too high to reach without steps. Then something said to me, why not try the ladder and the roof? The ladder itself was firmly secured to scaffolding with ropes, and I climbed up and got on to the roof to find there that although the slates, felting and boarding had been stripped, the men had conveniently lashed scaffold boards across the rafters, so that with the minimum of danger I could make my way across. I half thought that there might be a way through the roof, but a few judicious flashes with the torch showed that this wasn't on.

I walked across the scaffold boards to the other ladder and descended into the court-yard. There I found that there were two doors leading into the house. The amazing thing to me was that both of these doors had been left unlocked. I could only imagine that the housekeeper and the boss himself perhaps had probably thought that if the outside doors and windows were secure, what's it matter about the rest? They'd overlooked the fact that builders leave ladders around.

I did inspect carefully for some form of security device, just in case; but could see none. Going across the hall, I looked at the front door, and bless my stars I did, because this had a kind of primitive alarm which I imagined would have kicked up goodness knows what noise if I had set it off by forcing the door.

Before I had left France I had worked out which four of this collection I proposed to remove, so I now set about finding them. Not only had this man bought the paintings I had listed, but by what I could make out in the gloom he had bought a lot more. In fact, in the three main downstair rooms the pictures were hung so thickly on the walls that they looked like those old drawings of the early days of the Academy, or Dutch and Flemish studio interiors with the paintings arranged like stamps in tight regular rows.

I discovered the first two in the drawing-room. There was the Ben Marshall, entitled 'New Forest Ponies beneath a Tree', which I found later measured 28 by 36 inches; and on the wall opposite a good John Herring Senior 'A Boy with Black Horse and Ducks in a Farmyard' (this proved to be 28 by 34 inches). I got these two off the wall with no trouble. Then I thought a little camouflage was called for. I very carefully moved the paintings left so that both the gaps

were all but closed up and to an unaccustomed eye or a
quick glance the losses would to a high degree most
probably be hidden.

I carried the Marshall and Herring out into the hall and
went on a further ramble. In what was obviously the study I
picked up the one I believe I was most after. It was a fine
John Ferneley of a 'Grey Hunter' (measurements of this
proved to be 14¾ by 19½ inches). I did my picture-moving
act again, and this time with only one gone, after my having
moved one three inches this way and another four inches
that way, etcetera, the loss was really not at all obvious.

I tried the dining-room, and there to the right of the
sideboard and rather hidden by a hideous high leather
screen was the other one I had had in mind: 'Newmarket
with Racehorses' by James Seymour (34½ by 41 inches).
Same routine: painting off wall, rearranged the rest, moved
screen and deception all set.

Now came the rather perilous part that was to follow. I
felt the only safe way to get these pictures out was up and
over the roof, for if I tackled the front door, off would go
the alarm, and by now I had discovered there was another
of these gadgets on the back-door. The windows were set
high and it was too far to jump down – certainly with an
Old Master or two in one's arms. So, grinning and bearing
it or rather them, I did four very tiring lifts up the ladder
out of the court-yard, along the scaffold boards, feeling
carefully with my feet to avoid going between the rafters,
and down the ladder the other side. The worst one was the
Seymour not only because of its size, but also because it was
in a very heavy ornate carved frame. By something after
midnight I had got the four pictures out.

Now began another piece of sweat, carrying the pictures
up to the car. This took the best part of an hour. Then,
keeping a good look out for any vehicles coming, I took the

paintings out of their frames and put them in the back of the car. The frames I broke up and put into the boot for disposal at a safe range. I then drove off back to the inn, covered the paintings with a couple of rugs and locked the car. The landlord had kindly lent me a key with which I now let myself in.

Making sure of dates the next morning, I found I had time to squander before meeting Robert. I decided I would spend the next fortnight therefore cruising round old haunts, spending a night or two here and there.

During these days I bought some big sheets of cardboard, a lot of tissue paper, and a large enough piece of canvas to wrap up the whole bundle; to make a slightly more impressive package I also got hold of some rug straps with a handle. I threw the frames into a quarry waste-tip, drawing a pile of rubbish over them — anyway this was at least sixty miles from where they had previously hung on the walls. Every day I watched the papers, but nothing appeared; the housekeeper probably needed her glasses changed.

Early in October I gave the Piccadilly Hotel a ring, as I had promised, and in a few moments I heard my transatlantic friend's voice. When I told him in guarded sentences the news he said:

"That's great, Charles. Now when can you bring them up to me?"

I glanced at my watch and saw that it was just short of two o'clock and I was about fifty-five miles from London. I told him I could be with him between four and five.

The journey up was delayed a bit by convoys of lorries but I was nevertheless parking the car in St James's Square by about four thirty. I took out my somewhat cumbersome bundle and walked up and across Jermyn Street into Piccadilly and, waiting for my chance, crossed and entered the hotel. I asked reception and they gave me the room number of my friend, which was on the third floor. In a few minutes I was knocking at his door. In a matter of seconds (he must have been sitting like a jumping-jack) it opened and he gripped me excitedly by the arm. "Oh, Charles, this is just great." He shut the door and I noticed that he locked it. For a moment my red light blinked on again. Was I being done for a Charley, literally? Then, as he turned, he said:

"We don't want any intruders now, Charles, because I guess I'm not sure about your export regulations. I know my customs rules but not yours. I like to keep these things private."

He sounded fairly genuine, but I kept the red light going. I undid the bundle and as I brought out the pictures one after the other I could see I had landed what he wanted. It was quite impressive that he could identify the painter of 'A Boy with Black Horse and Ducks in a Farmyard', also the Marshall, with which he was absolutely thrilled. I had to jog his memory over the Seymour, but with a little prodding he got the 'Grey Hunter' as by Ferneley. He went over the pictures carefully, examining practically every square inch of the paint surface, and looked at the backs.

"Well, Charles, I've got no worries there at all. Now how much change do I get out of my hundred thousand dollars?"

I said: "Well, I'm not very good at this working across into other currencies. As far as I am concerned, to break even I've got to charge you £12,200."

He did a quick mental gymnastic or two and then replied:

"That leaves me plenty in pocket. I'll tell you something, you make that around £13,000; as I said, I am putting in the expenses, Charles. I'm real pleased, and I hope we're going to do more business in the future."

He went over to a thick black leather brief-case that was on the table beside the bed, took out a key on a long chain and unlocked the heavy brass fastening. He took out an impressive wad of hundred dollar bills, and very expertly and quickly he counted their equivalent of £13,000. I was in a slight predicament because that amount of bills is pretty thick and I hadn't exactly brought a suitcase with me. So, in the end, I had to rather ignominiously split them up round my various pockets. One pile went inside my coat; another wad into the hip-pocket of my trousers; and other bundles into the outside pockets of my coat and down into my side trouser pockets. Robert laughed, watching this performance. "Charles, you look like a walking Fort Knox."

"Well, I rather feel that way," I replied.

As I tried to pat the bulges in my clothes flatter, he asked:

"Now have you an address I can write to because I feel we are going to have to keep in contact?"

I told him that at the moment I hadn't a permanent address, as ever since the war I had more or less been wandering round. Finally it was left that I should contact him. He gave me a heavily embossed card on which were all the details. I told him that maybe in a few years I would be visiting the States and that I would most certainly look him up.

*   *   *

Christmas 1952 was not my first one in my self-imposed exile, but in a strange way this moment in the year's calendar seemed to affect me more deeply that year than previously. My little house momentarily felt almost like a prison. Memory, sentiment and nostalgia turned the air into a suffocatingly stiff mixture.

As I went out into the town to buy the necessaries, I was

jostling my way through family groups with children gaz-ing glitter-eyed into the decorated shops. Tinsel fancies flashed in the passing car lights. I felt that if it were only for two or three days, I must take myself away. Yet I didn't really want to go back to London or England. I ran through some of the possibilities, and as I did so, I realized that every now and then the loner can let the batteries run flat.

It wasn't until the day before Christmas Eve that in a form of desperation I packed a bag and got into the car and drove at first I wasn't quite sure where. By lunch-time I found myself away to the north passing through Romorantin; after this I caught a brief glance of the stately façade of the Château at Cheverny. I stopped for lunch at a small café in the Place du Château at Blois, perched on top of its hill. After a poor omelette and a poor glass of wine I drove on through Vendôme and then up to Châteaudun and there caught a glimpse of the sign to Chartres.

As things do, this in a moment evoked an image that held out some sort of promise. Something clicked in the mechanism of my brain and a curtain rolled away. Perhaps I really am a chameleon. Almost instantly everything seemed to look different. Was I falling victim to some strange mental trap for the solitary?

It is one thing to go down the street and carry on restricted relationships with shopkeepers which get little further than being bid good morning, a remark on the weather, a comment on rising prices or words on the quality. It is another matter to have a relationship of closeness with some one. With this you can be part of their life, and they a part of yours.

With me, alcohol is not the only stimulant that can bring on a state of inebriation. Fantasy thoughts, effects, sur-roundings, all kinds of strange happenings can become stimulants which set me off. That afternoon it was the sign to Chartres.

As I approached the town, I could see the two needle spires of this one and only building. I was fortunate that I found a hotel, and a good one, at the first try. I got myself booked in and the car garaged away. It was only four o'clock and there was still sufficient light for a walk across to the cathedral.

It stood there just as my last memory had left it, unique in its conception and with the decoration that it held. As with Bourges, here was a whole book of creation carved across the stonework. Inside I was just in time to catch the last of the daylight through those incomparable windows; harmonies of colour brought into life by transmitted light. Looking across the interior, it was studded here and there by long candles, the flames of which burnt with star-like sharpness, each illuminating a tiny patch of the fabric of Chartres, and laying a light golden haze on a few bowed heads.

Outside again, I stood with my back leaning against a wall opposite and watched the last vestiges of the daylight soften the hard edges of the towers, the buttresses and columns, until the whole form of the building seemed to change from something in the third dimension to just a vast dark two-dimensional silhouette cut into the tones of the approaching night-sky.

I felt that I was letting myself get into a dangerous, almost maudlin state. At the same time I didn't think that there was much I could do about it; in fact, I wasn't sure that I wanted to do anything about it. It was deliciously relaxing, perhaps because I was quite simply entering the world of normal people. I walked back to the hotel and went up to my room; and for the first time for many months decided to change for dinner. Taking off a somewhat battered Harris tweed jacket and a near-worn-out pair of corduroys, I put out a dark grey suit. I found myself choosing the shirt I was to wear with some thought and trying several ties till I got just the one I wanted. I even had an evening shave – unheard of with my colouring to get a six o'clock shadow.

Downstairs the bar was cosy and warm with several secluded booths where it was possible to enjoy one's drink in peace, a method which I greatly favour. As I sipped a long glass of vermouth, I immersed myself in my well-thumbed booklet on Chartres. At heart I am an inveterate tourist. I love to go to a place, look at it, and then read about it. At the same time I run through my mind a kind of film of what I have seen and fit it against the commentary I am reading. I had become so engrossed with this pastime that I had not noticed that the seat opposite to me had been taken.

It wasn't until I finished the booklet and looked up that I found myself somewhat rudely and blatantly staring at the occupant. A soft gentle voice said, "I hope you haven't been keeping this for someone, but all the other places were taken. I didn't like to disturb you."

Her eyes had no hint of brashness or deception; they merely underlined the sincerity of the way in which she had spoken.

I replied, "Of course not. No, I'm alone." Then realizing that I was on the way to behaving rather gauchely, I pulled myself up. Fumbling for a cigarette, I did a foolishly obvious gambit by offering her one. She took it with the merest wisp of a smile, and then I held out a lighter which shook more than it should have done. Both of us almost instantaneously started to speak and then stopped. I made a little gesture with my hands and said, "Please, after you."

She gave a tiny laugh and went on, "I think we both

must be a long way away from home." Then after a pause and for seemingly no reason at all, "It's what I've always wanted," she said.

I knew that within me a piece of my make-up which for a long time I had kept forcibly suppressed was making one great break for liberty. Feebly, what I had hoped and imagined was the stronger part of me, said . . . 'Don't be silly, you will wreck everything you have planned and worked for'. But the freedom-seeking character whispered . . . 'why not relax, let yourself go'. This was parried with . . . 'it could be a trap'. But the member for liberation just sniffed. The other side tried once more, and then knew perhaps it would be best to give the other lad a Christmas present of his own way, but whispered . . . 'mind you, I'm off again immediately after Boxing Day'.

So it started.

She was on the run from a family break-up. The tortured tensions of discord between her mother and her father had finally driven her away, at least for a week or two. She had nipped off from the ancestral home in Worcestershire in her small car. First of all she had tried London, but found there she was all the time bumping into acquaintances and gossip-tongued friends and it gave her no escape. Five days ago she had crossed to Calais and tried Paris; but the very first evening had run into somebody she knew.

At this point I signalled the waiter over and our glasses were refilled. I cannot imagine what she must have thought was going on in my mind. It was so long since I had had an intimate brush with another person. But for myself, I know that as I looked across at her a spot of magic did happen.

She had one of those faces in which perhaps there is no particular strikingly single beautiful feature, yet when all that was there was brought together it made a picture which I found extraordinarily enticing. The mouth although quite small had an inviting softness. The eyes, a kind of wary grey, flecked I suppose with just a little blue, looked at me with a calmness and a certain quality of penetrative analysis which I didn't find unpleasant. Her name, although it was only the Christian one she gave me, was Charlotte. When I gave her mine I found myself for a moment in a dilemma. The careful side of my being was still holding a little bit of a rein, and said . . . 'don't say Edward'. Anyhow that wasn't my name either. In fact, I had almost in a dotty way lost track of what my real name was. So in the end, rather weakly, I fell back on Charles. With it I matched my story of being a student of art and architecture. When she heard all this she gave a laugh and said, "It sounds as though we're twins. Charles and Charlotte."

The chemistry of lonely like souls when they meet was beginning to work. After another drink we went into dinner. A sympathetic head waiter led us to a private table in one corner. There was a quite memorable rough duck pâté, after which we had poached trout swathed in an exquisite sauce, and then Charlotte chose fruit and cheese, and I followed. From an ample cheeseboard we both selected three or four wedges of different kinds. We pulled off small bunches of grapes, took a pear and an apple each. Then rather lightheadedly Charles, for he certainly wasn't acting like Edward, ordered another bottle of wine, a light white to complement the fruit and cheese.

We were about half-way through this part of the meal when quite suddenly she put her left hand across the table and on top of mine. With the other hand she lifted her glass and said, "Charles, let's have a wonderful few days . . ." punctuating the remark at the end with a very long pause . . . Then she put her glass to her lips and whispered, "Shall we?"

The only other thing I remember about that night before

Christmas Eve in Chartres was standing rather self-consciously in front of Charlotte by her room door and saying, "Goodnight . . . dear." The part of this moment that I really remember was when she, without saying anything, reached up and put her arms round my neck and pulled my face down towards her. She left the merest touch of her lips just at the corner of my mouth and it was followed by the most silent kiss noise I ever remember.

The next morning we entered for breakfast as seasoned friends. Afterwards we walked out into the square and went to the cathedral. I don't know what I was giving her, but I know that she was giving me a tonic which was doing wonders. It was chipping off and rubbing away the jaded areas that I hadn't even known about. It was, I knew, giving me love; and this was a tricky one. This was something I had not catered for with the life of Mr Hood.

As I looked back on that Christmas Eve and the Christmas Day and the Boxing Day that followed, it is only a memory of joy.

After the lunch on Christmas Eve I excused myself and went searching through the shops, looking for something. In the end, not very original, some lace, two silk scarves and rather daringly a bottle of very expensive perfume which I knew I liked and hoped that she would. I had even bought pretty paper and bright ribbons to wrap up these offerings.

After dinner that night we retired away to her room to share whatever there was in these borrowed hours.

Christmas morning I was up before the call. I put on my dressing-gown and gathered up the parcels; then I went down the passage and knocked at Charlotte's door. She also was up and was sitting at the dressing-table as I walked in following her call. She was just putting the last touches to some parcels. When she saw my packages, for just a moment a sadness flicked across her face, but this was quickly pushed away by a smile of great joy. Of course she loved the lace; the scarves were just what she wanted; and the perfume was adorable. For her part she had found a box of the cigars she had noticed I was smoking, a large box, much too large I thought because they were expensive. With it a very fine deep green satin tie, which she said, "I think, Charles, would suit you even better than the red one you were wearing the night we met."

Boxing Day had come and gone. I knew as I crept back to my own room at about four in the morning of the 27th that I was feeling a sensation that was akin to the finish of some long forgotten four-day leave in the war. It must end.

I have only one real joy in life and that is beauty. I don't mind whether it is a painting, a work from one of the great ebénistes of the eighteenth century, a carving in the milk-white Carrara, an exquisite piece of Meissen, a beautiful boy or girl. I have only one real sadness – that my make-up is fickle; having squeezed the maximum of satisfaction from my thing of beauty, if it is a work of art, I sell it; if it is one of the other two, I travel on.

Works of art sometimes I can hold on to for a while before I pass them on. Works of creative craftsmanship from the hands of genius give me some part of the struggling joy with which they were brought into being. These things make no more demand than appreciation. Others, such as Charlotte, I knew I wanted really just as much and more. But I felt in the strange recesses of myself that they must be left. Charlotte and I in these few days had reached and found something of love. But now I must journey on.

Although I had gone to bed so late, I awoke before seven. I dressed quickly, packed my bag, wrote a very brief note to Charlotte, and as I went down the passage slipped it under her door. I then hurried down to reception where I managed to get a somewhat sleepy-eyed porter to go and find someone who could make out my bill. By half past seven I was away heading towards the south.

Back home once more, the little house like its owner seemed to have had an injection of fresh life. What before had begun to feel stagnant and constricting was now warm and friendly and had me working away with my index books. I had previously just started work on another one which was a kind of almanac reaching as far as possible into the future with regular events, social, fashionable and sport-wise. Using this, I hoped to forecast with a fair degree of accuracy who would be where and when. There was also another slightly slimmer tome. This was a highly selective address book. For instance, if I looked up a particular titled or rich person, this book would show me their principal home or seat, and other houses.

Sometime ago I had made an arrangement with a news-agent in Paris for a regular supply of the main gossip magazines of France, Italy, Germany and Britain. Period-icals such as *The Tatler* and similar orientated publications can provide an extraordinary amount of whereabouts infor-mation. These I was in the habit of collecting at roughly monthly intervals; if I was away longer my newsagent friend would store them for me.

By the use of a few diagrams I found that I could plot the round of the 'in' people to a fair degree. Many of them stick tightly to their routine. There are certain events at which it is mandatory to be seen. Often, conveniently for me, they also travel with quite a large part of their staff: chauffeurs, maids, men-servants. If the likes of myself really do their home-work, they can move around like peripatetic crop-pickers.

1953 held promise, because of two social events which cut across the general pattern, and by so doing they would bring a certain amount of upper-crust chaos. I've noticed that when chaos enters, normal routine carefulness tends to evaporate. The first of these 'five-star' events, which might actually have been looked upon as a rehearsal for the second, was a fairy-tale marriage in Luxembourg. This was between Prince Jean, heir to the throne there, and his childhood friend, Princess Josephine-Charlotte of Belgium. Prince Jean had led a varied life; he had gone to school in England and during the war had fought with the Irish Guards. To the wedding undoubtedly would come a very considerable concourse of the quality.

But much more so would the turn-out be for the next event. This was to be the Coronation of Queen Elizabeth II on June 2nd in Westminster Abbey. Here was a must for the 'crème de la crème' of Europe and even to an extent of the world.

By keeping a steady eye on the periodicals and a select number of the dailies, I was very soon able to build up a list of the guests who would be coming and in some cases even to find out the dates of their stay and where.

I myself quite naturally would not be going over to London for this. I felt there could be more profit in being elsewhere.

In April I packed a couple of large suit-cases, put the directories into a brief-case which I could lock securely, and, fastening up the little house, I set off to the south of France. I intended to creep round the mass of the Alps by the coast road which runs along from Nice, Monaco, Menton through Alassio and Savona to Genoa.

It was in a village about twenty kilometres to the east of this port that I was hoping to pick up an Italian equivalent of my friend in Alsace. It is quite a long and tricky business not only finding the targets, but also the safe disposal people. These latter gentlemen have to be discreet to the limit, as well as of the mood to give one a reasonable return for labours incurred.

Once clear of Genoa, I motored away up into the hills and found that my purist Italian was being somewhat strained amongst the villagers who spoke a very distinct dialect of the extreme north. For me, Italy and its people has an extraordinary pacifying effect; I find it is almost impossible to get cross with a people who so obviously like to leave things until tomorrow. A glass of wine in an Italian café lasts even longer than one in France or Spain. And provided you don't want to work too hard afterwards, many of their strong reds have much to commend them.

It took three days to run down the character I was seeking. Then it took me the whole of one afternoon, that evening, and practically until midnight to get to the point with him. For long hours we both stuck to the themes of our feigned personalities; he as a respectable antique dealer; I as a student of the arts. We must each have pursued almost every known gambit to reach our individual intents without at the same time exposing what we didn't want to. At last we did make a break-through, and then it became much simpler.

Yes, he would handle the paintings, but nothing too big in size – big ones were too much trouble, too difficult to pack (or hide, I thought). He did not want anything larger than about twenty-eight by thirty-six inches. Moreover he was adamant that I should understand that it would be his judgement against mine as to authenticity; to this I gave only a murmured noise of assent. Before we parted he also insisted I must not write to him or telephone. On a small scrap of paper he scribbled down a series of three sets of dates and told me that in the next twelve months he would be at his home except for these periods.

The next morning I drove back out of the mountains to

pick up again the coast road that went on down towards the south through Carrara, with the bare white faces of the quarries, harsh in the noon sunlight, along by Viareggio, to Lucca, where I paused for the night. I had never been to this enchanting place before, with its immense wall surrounding the old town; so wide is the wall that a road runs along the top; and there must surely be more churches here, I supposed, than in any other town of comparable size.

After dinner I sat mulling over an idea which had been coming to me gradually: that it would be a good plan to have a second hideaway, in case it should ever be needed. I had thought about Spain, even parts of northern Europe; but I had come to the conclusion that the atmosphere which could well be best would be somewhere in the high belly of Italy, and I had mentally picked a triangle of Bologna, Ravenna and Florence in which to search.

The following day I drove east from Lucca, past Pistóia and into Florence for the next night. Oh, how I wished I could have had the hideout here. But something told me that a city was not the place for what I had in mind. Yet I don't think anywhere I have ever visited so wrapped me in the almost overpowering majesty of the Renaissance as Florence. It has been said, I believe, that Florence is not a city of hundreds and thousands of houses, but rather one big museum.

Howbeit, pause at that moment I must not; the date of that coronation in England was creeping up. I wanted to have my second place ready. With that done I could hie up to the north and the social heart of Europe from where so many were going to be absent.

Finally I did find that for which I was searching, although it wasn't within the original triangle; instead it came within a rough square bounded by Florence, Ravenna, Pesaro and Arezzo. I found it with the help of a glass of wine and the priest of the small village. We had chatted together for some time when I told him what I was actually looking for. He thought he knew just the place he said, and he even kindly said he would show me. He broke into his rest-time to do this, and led me down a narrow alley way, under a series of arches between two close-standing buildings and round behind the church to a small two-storeyed building, the bottom floor of which he told me was used only twice a year for some meetings to do with the church. He explained that on the top part were two rooms and a wash-place (these had been used by an American artist for a short time just after the war). For the last three years it had been empty, he continued, and he knew the church would be only too willing to rent it to me at a very reasonable sum indeed. He got the key from a house near by, and we mounted the stone stairs that went up the side of the building which was made of soft creamy stone gently abraded by quite a few centuries. I had noted the pleasant contrast of the roof, which was of dark red tiles.

At the top of the stairs was a double door rather like those mostly found in stables. The upper portion held the lock part. The priest had a little trouble with the old key sticking at first, but eventually it worked all right, and we decided this could soon be rectified. The bottom half of the door was held in place inside by one big bolt. Beyond was a minute hall, and off this were two rooms. The larger had obviously been the studio, as it still bore signs of paint-brush marks on the walls, and lying about in the fireplace were a number of squeezed-up empty tubes and an empty bottle that looked as if it had probably held linseed oil. There were two windows: the smaller of the two looked straight on to the back of the church; from the other I could see the roofs of the village and rising up behind them in the distance a lovely view studded with olive trees and dotted here and there with what were obviously little cream-walled houses, all receding away it seemed to melt at last into the blue haze of the sky. The other room across the hall had been the bedroom, and off this was a little wash-place. It had a tap and a sink and a what could be described as an economic usual of great antiquity. Cooking arrangements? There seemed to be none. There was a stained marble shelf in the wash-place which showed signs of having had fat spilt on it. But I felt this place would do. I would only need the minimum of furniture, and a gas or paraffin cooker. Anything else I could think of would gradually improve its amenities.

The priest said he would get a lease made out, and he would meet me at the café at the same time the next day. I asked him if he would like three or six months' or a year's rent in advance. He was happy with six months.

We met as arranged and my new friend had the lease ready. I gave him the six months' rent. I asked him where he thought I could get some small pieces of furniture. At once he produced the name of a friend who ran a small second-hand store half-way down the hill leading out of the village. From this eager source I procured a bed, a table, two chairs, an easy chair, a small hanging cupboard, and a chest of drawers, also some strips of carpet. Before these were moved in the priest found me a willing lady who gave my new apartment a most thorough scrubbing-out.

A trip to Florence through the mountains produced a mattress, bed-clothes, towels, oil-cooker, cutlery, china, glass, and a small portable gas-light and a packet of candles.

Italy, taken all over, was still panting from the extreme trauma that it had been through during the last twenty years or more. Although then the thefts of works of art were on nothing like the scale they were to reach in the future, valuable pieces of silver, carved objects and paintings were starting to get on the move and to disappear. It may sound queer coming from me, but I felt it was a pity churches were amongst the victims. I know that one of the first things I acquired was the Van Eyck, which had, admittedly, come originally from a church, but I have salved my conscience, to a degree, by telling myself that I didn't actually take it from a church. I took it from Ernst. And where had Ernst got it from? Anyway I had long since decided that stealing from churches was not for me. Nevertheless, churches apart, I was very interested in all the other goings on, and my small flat behind the church in that village gave me a listening-post.

*   *   *

During the last week of May and first week of June Mr Hood did himself quite comfortably moving around from stately schloss to charming château and elsewhere. I managed to gather seven paintings of worth. They all conformed to the size limit of my contact near Genoa. All this did entail quite a lot of driving, because then it would have been a bit tricky to come down from Germany straight through Austria. I did not think it was worth all the extra border formalities going across Switzerland, so I had to go back into France and come along the southern coast road again. For camouflage I had fallen back on my amateur artist's status. At the house in France I kept a goodly supply of paints, brushes, bottles, and a number of canvases of different sizes; thus when I arrived at the frontier of Italy the seven paintings looked no more valuable than seven ready-primed artist's canvases, and they, of course, did not relate size-wise to the paintings they concealed.

Things had worked out well; for when I arrived in the village of the 'dealer' near Genoa I was well inside one of his 'at home' periods. I waited until dusk and then I made my call. He was alone, as I imagined he nearly always was. I could see the packing method impressed him, and he was even more impressed when the paintings were on the table in front of him. Giving them a meticulous going over, even in two cases with a form of microscope, he missed nothing, as far as I could see. All was successful, and the result was soon duly transported by me over the mountains to the Swiss bank.

Matters were now looking quite appreciably better, and I saw a period of further indulgences approaching. In fact, I am almost ashamed to say, I was to make the most of it, and the gratification I discovered took me through to the latter part of 1956. Three years, I know, but it was well worth it. I travelled largely for enjoyment, and I was not always alone. First of all, there was the exploration of Italy, something I had wanted to do for years; and this place can lead to numerous satisfactions. I did make returns to the French base, as well as several visits to England. And I met a number of new people in the various countries who were to prove useful to me in the future. It is surprising how easily at a social get-together, once one has got through the doors, one is accepted and becomes part of the scene, and how freely, what I would call top classified information is bandied around by some well-lined people. Very seldom was I asked embarrassing questions about who I was, where I came from or what any of my history was. Indeed, I know some felt they knew quite a bit about me, and greeted me as an old friend. I did, of course, feed them what I wanted them 'to know'.

Going back to the profit side of my business, however, in 1956 I picked up one interesting little piece from a small museum in the Naples area. I don't know how many museums there are in Italy, but it seemed as though I could spend year after year visiting a different one each day. They ranged in size from small establishments, sometimes attached to churches and housing the odd pieces of carving and examples of excavated pottery, to vast galleries like the Uffizzi and some of the places in Rome. It is true, to lift something from one of the small places like I did that day, was rather perhaps taking an unfair advantage, because generally they seemed to have just one man on the door selling the tickets, and that was all.

This one held a number of rather interesting early paintings. I wandered round entranced by the essential purity which some of these Italian artists could achieve. They eschewed the conceits and fashions, and their statements had a sincerity. There were about half a dozen rooms in the museum, and there didn't seem a sign of a guardian except for the one who had sold me a ticket. He was happy enough that I should have paid my entrance, and lounged back in his chair admiring the view across the square through a wide-open door.

In the last of the rooms I came to, which was the one farthest away from him, hanging in the middle of one of the walls was a small portrait, a head and shoulders of a dignified and serious girl; her age difficult to judge, but if it were today I should have thought her between nineteen and twenty. She was dressed in a plain robe, with a creamy-yellow sash round her shoulders, and round her neck several necklaces. Her hair was gathered tightly. But it was the eyes that caught me. They were calm and looked out of the painting and over my right shoulder. I almost involuntarily stepped to the right trying to meet her gaze. The whole I was to find measured only about eight by ten inches. Although no title had been put to the picture nor any artist mentioned, I felt it could be by Del Sarto. There was his touch about it. There was also a feel of Raphael, but I felt strongly it was more likely the former painter.

I knew this one must come away with me. Although it was small, it was still a little large to hide under my light-weight jacket. Returning to the room I had come out of previously, I found I had overlooked a doorway. I went over to this and tried the latch. It lifted and I found that the door opened quite silently on to a small enclosed backyard. On further surreptitious investigation, I discovered a door on the other side of the yard opened out into a roadway. Opposite was the blank wall of a large religious establishment, and this was about fourteen feet high with no overlooking windows; on the museum side, as far as I could see, there were no windows looking out towards the road either. Just inside the yard next to this exit door there were several sheets of corrugated iron leaning against the wall, with odd planks and builders' debris.

Quietly I desert-booted my way back into the room where the little portrait was, and gave it the routine scrutiny behind. There was nothing to see except an old piece of bent twisted wire hung over a flat-headed nail. I lifted off the girl, walked back into the other room, through the door into the yard, and lent her against the wall underneath the builders' materials. Went back, closed the door and sauntered round the other rooms for about five minutes, and then went out to pass quite a long time of day with the doorkeeper. In fact, whilst doing so I even went through a little pantomime of taking off my jacket and laying it for a while on the back of a chair as I talked to him. I took out a packet of cigarettes, offered him one, took one myself, lit up. I took up the jacket, laid it across my arm, and with a friendly farewell walked out into the square.

I fetched my car, found the narrow roadway behind the museum, stopped by the doorway and got out. The door opened just as easily from the outside; I leant in and picked up the picture from its temporary hiding-place and was back in the car and moving off within not much over the minute.

It was a few months before I could dispose of the little girl to my Genoese contact. He was delighted with her, although he did not altogether go along with my assumption regarding Del Sarto. He wouldn't say anything. But I gathered from the sum he somewhat guardedly and unwillingly counted out for me that she must be good. I never did find out what he did with the paintings; but I can only imagine he must have been on one or other of the smuggling circuits which were beginning to build up in Italy.

It was shortly after this episode that I thought I had better give Robert, my American client, a call. I didn't want to let that association get too cool. Whilst staying in a hotel in Milan I squandered what seemed like a ransom in lira to telephone his number. Fortunately I put it in personal, because when the operator got through she found he was out and wouldn't be back until ten that night. At ten the operator got me the call again and I heard the warm friendly tones I remembered from Bourges coming through clearly. The very first thing he said was:

"Well, Charles, you must be a thought-reader, because . . . gee . . . for some time I've been saying why can't I get in touch with that guy? Has he got nowhere I can call him or write?"

I hummed, and passed this one by, and then he went on:

"Now look, Charles, I'm finding myself with more wall space. I want you to fill this for me. Now don't be startled. I haven't gone off these horse pictures. But this little room we have had built . . . well, it isn't all that small . . . it's a kind of lounge that I've had specially done for my wife. She's wanted a place to entertain her friends . . . well we've stuck it on the end of the house like a wing . . . and it's real nice. There's a little sunken garden out in front of it. It's real pretty. I'm going to give you quite an order this time. . . . You don't know my wife, but someday you are going to have the pleasure of meeting her. Well, someways back she's got Spanish in her blood . . . and what we're doin' with this room . . . it's being decked out with real Cordoba leather upholstery, and she's been really shopping around. Where we're stuck is . . . we want some Spanish pictures. Now, Charles, none of this modern stuff. I know what she'd really like . . . she wants something to give it class . . . some early portraits of . . . oh, I guess I don't mind who . . . royalty if you like. She's always been telling me that one line of her family goes back very close to the palace there in Madrid or wherever it is. I guess there's room for six portraits. Gee, it sounds like I'm reeling off a grocer's list. Also she's got a room off our bedroom which she uses for sewing, maybe resting up and doing her writing; I know she'd just love one of those flower pictures and still life things. You just have a look round, Charles, and see if you can rustle up a couple. Now I know that this is a big order . . . You give me a call . . . say before Christmas. How about that, Charles?"

After my having said I would do what I could and ring him as suggested, and then a few pleasantries, rather to my relief he rang off. I felt I had to gather my wits. I had had the odd trip to Spain. But frankly, to a fair old degree, much of their painting had still to be ferreted out. This was going to need quite a bit of book-work and some scratching to see where they could possibly be. It seemed time to go back again to France. I paid up another six months' rent to my neighbourly priest, locked up the flat and motored away.

When I arrived back at the French base, the first thing I did after I had dumped my luggage was to nip up to Paris to pick up a large pile of periodicals and papers the news-agent had been holding for me.

I got all these back and laid them out, pulled down a mass of reference books and found that I was going to be in for quite a task. Robert had really come up with a tough one. Almost automatically I scratched out El Greco, Velazquez and Goya. There are precious few of these lying around outside galleries and if I were to walk into the Prado and scoop up a half dozen, and pretend I was a removal man, the sleepiest guards were going to sense something was wrong. No, I felt that there was a better way round it than any such scheme. Let's give the man something that probably no one else over there in the States would be likely to have.

As I've said, the documentation on Spanish pictures in general, and for that matter Portuguese too, is maybe the weakest for any group in Europe outside of Scandinavia. But, thanks to the prodding and guidance from André, I had been able to amass some useful leads for this field. Italy had Vasari, who was one of the early art historians; Spain had Palomino. He was born near Cordoba in 1653; and although he was a fairly successful painter in oils and to a lesser extent in fresco, Palomino is today best remembered for his comments on art and artists. In two of his large volumes he gives material about some two hundred painters and sculptors who were working in Spain from the time of Ferdinand the Catholic until the end of the reign of Philip IV. An abridged version of these books in Spanish was published in 1742 in London and later was translated into English. The original volumes had more than their share of mistakes. But for all that there is a large amount of information. They remained the principal source until a more accurate work was produced by Cean Bermudez.

When I had worked out a possible short list of portrait painters, and flower and still life artists, the next step, which was considerably harder, was to find out where good examples could be found.

On thinking this problem through, at first I was not enthusiastic. It is one thing to behave in an uncivilized manner in the rest of Europe, but over the Pyrenees it could be a very different proposition. There were several ifs and buts about it. My normal information services didn't seem to be shedding much light on the scene. My business is not really something that you can go asking questions about off the man in the street. I had a row of lights flashing bright strong red against any idea of roaring up to one of those great haciendas and doing a lift-off. Even if I got past this part I had serious doubts about the ease with which I would be able to get them out of Spain. I had sharp memories of the efficient policing.

However, I didn't want to lose Robert. I was learning about collectors, and he promised to be something quite special. A flash did come at last. I could see how this operation could be done, but in a totally different way. In Spain I would be legitimate. What I had to do was to find some paintings elsewhere and take them into Spain with me and pose as a bona fide dealer. What kind of paintings would dealers in Spain be keen on? I asked myself. About the only guidelines I had on this point were from history. It seemed that the Venetians and the early Flemish had held attraction for that part of the world.

Step one, I thought, would be to change the Renault, which was now getting a bit past it. This time I got a new Peugeot, which was to serve me well. I packed the odd suitcases and also my amateur painter's outfit. I had increased this. Apart from the sketching-easel, bags with bottles and brushes, I now included three of those gadgets which could be used for carrying two pictures and keeping them about two inches away from each other. I put in some ten assorted canvases, a roll of canvas, a tin of tacks, the stapler, a hammer, and other odds and ends.

*　　*　　*

It was July 1957 when I set out on this next saga. I'm a bit of a strange one because each of these jaunts becomes an adventure. The thing I have to remember is that they are adventures that could have some rather sour nasty edges to them; I've got to keep awake and alert so that I don't go and do anything stupid in the same category as when I yanked the Degas across the Channel in a suitcase.

Anew I entered Italy via the south coast road through Genoa and from there I cut away to the north east via Tortona. I went through Milan, and stopped off for the night at Bergamo. Continuing the next morning through Brescia and so into the hunting-ground that I had chosen, I found a little inn between Verona and Vicenza and booked in for five nights to start with whilst I went on a recce.

Venice I had counted out because it would be too tricky a place to indulge in any form of chase in. I thought of the mainland behind it. I was getting to know Italy fairly well. The area stretched to Treviso in the east and across to Padua and Vicenza, the birthplace of the architect Andrea Palladio (1518–1580), I remembered. I also remembered that sadly the Gothic thirteenth century cathedral and a number of other important buildings had been savagely mauled in the war. Vicenza's population I reckoned as around the hundred thousand mark. Treviso was about an hour's run away and also had its cathedral, but this one had suffered from over-restoration.

The tour I was following in those five days covered nearly every road in the district. By the time I was finished I was well-coated in dust and well-bitten by insects; but I

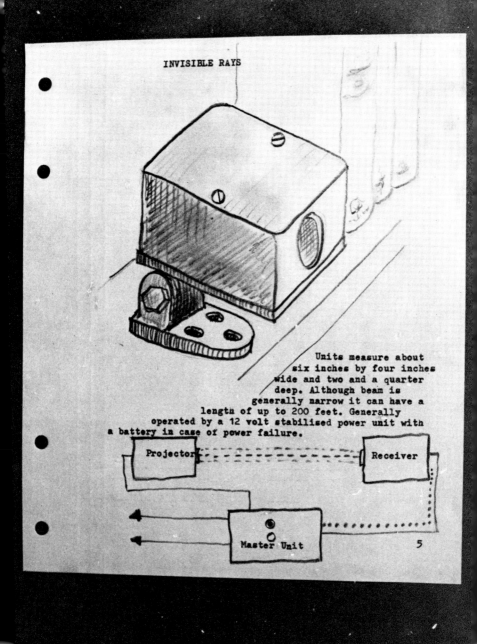

INVISIBLE RAYS

Units measure about
six inches by four inches
wide and two and a quarter
deep. Although beam is
generally narrow it can have a
length of up to 200 feet. Generally
operated by a 12 volt stabilised power unit with
a battery in case of power failure.

Projector   Receiver

Master Unit   5

Page from security file, showing working of photo-electric cell.

Specimen signatures. *Left* – Nicolas Maes; Gabriel Metsu; Anthonis Mor;
Peeter Neeffs; Jean Baptiste Oudry; Nicolas Poussin; Rembrandt van Ryn;
Sir Peter Paul Rubens. *Right* – Hans Memling; Jean Baptiste Monneyer;
George Morland; Bernaert van Orley; Pietro Perugino; Raphael; Salvator
Rosa; Andrea del Sarto.

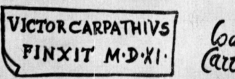

Specimen signatures. *Top to bottom* – Pieter Aertsen & Francesco Albani; Albrecht Altdorfer & Alessandro Allori; Sofonisba Anguiscola; Antonello da Messina; Hendrik Avercamp & Giovanni Bellini; Hendrik van Balen & Nicholas Berchem; Ferdinand Bol & Paul Bril; Hieronymus Bosch & Pieter Brueghel the Younger; Agnolo Bronzino; Vittore Carpaccio & Lodovico Carraci.

'Deux chaises dans le jardin' by Pierre Bonnard. Stolen with the Gauguin 'Nature morte...' in 1970. Value together £250,000. Reward offered of £17,500, for the return of both.

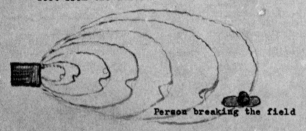

Unit measures less than eight
inches high by five and a half
wide and three inches deep.

The protective field reaches out about thirty
feet from the unit.

Person breaking the field   6

Notes on microwave intrusion detection in security file.

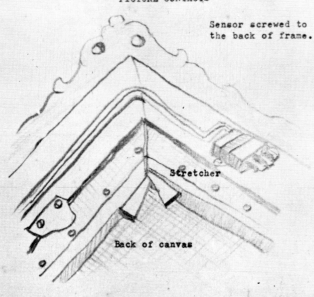

Sensor screwed to
the back of frame.

Stretcher

Back of canvas

A more difficult device to defeat.
It is fixed to the frame but is also in
contact with the canvas or panel. The
raised arm guards against complete removal
from the wall.

8

Electronic picture contacts in security file.

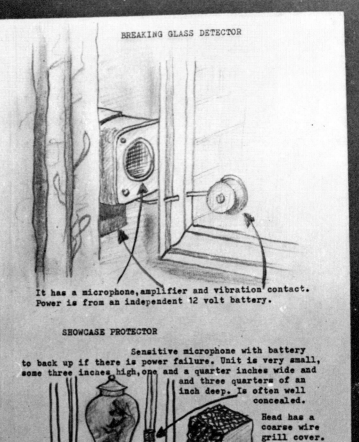

It has a microphone, amplifier and vibration contact.
Power is from an independent 12 volt battery.

SHOWCASE PROTECTOR

Sensitive microphone with battery
to back up if there is power failure. Unit is very small,
some three inches high, one and a quarter inches wide and
and three quarters of an
inch deep. Is often well
concealed.

Head has a
coarse wire
grill cover.

11

Security file: detector for breaking glass.

did have five items I wanted; two very charming Madonnas with Child and three allegorical paintings in the rich translucent colourful style of Titian and his followers. I had spent the last afternoon in the foot-hills in a secluded spot carrying out my sandwich technique to disguise the pictures for onward routing.

Leaving the inn at which I had been staying, I crossed the country for a bit till I got on to the main road to Padua, and then started to drive away to the south, thinking to spend a short spell at the apartment down there. When I was well on the road to Ferrara, for no special reason I cut away to the left. After some half hour's drive I found that I was approaching the coast. There was the most wonderful view looking out across the Adriatic. The water had that quality sometimes attained by the sea around the east coast of Sicily. (I recall once standing high up at Taormina and looking down into the seas there which were blue and opaque, close to the colour of pale ultramarine ash.) The heat of the afternoon sun was so baking the landscape this particular day that even the dry stretches of tanned grass seemed to be driven up into the columns of vapour which wavered and made the whole scene quiver with weird animation. I stopped the car and got out, took a long pull at a bottle of Pellegrino water and an equally long pull at a thin cigar. I walked away over a slight rise in the ground. As I surmounted this, I saw tucked away near the top of a valley a small but clearly expensive villa. It had in front a garden which was sporting a blaze of red flowers. The immediate area at the sides and the back was studded with those tall thin cypresses without which the Italian scene would seem bare. I went back to the car and got my binoculars and then returned and sat down on a flat rock which just allowed me to see the villa but hid me. For some half an hour on and off I watched, training the glasses on to

11—MOAAT • •

one window after another, both the doors, and what I imagined was the garage. No sign could I see of anyone. In fact, all the windows were tight-shut and so were the doors.

Looking at my watch, I saw that it was a little before four o'clock; it was going to be a long wait for the dusk. But I had a feeling that it could be worth it. I went back to the car and fetched my bottle of Pellegrino and a lump of sausage and some bread which I had left over from a picnic lunch. Making myself reasonably comfortable, this time sitting on the ground and leaning back against the rock, I could still make out what was happening below me.

About half past five a ramshackle baby Fiat came up the drive, loosening a spiral of dust. It drew up in front of the villa and through the glasses I saw a thick-set swarthy fellow get out. His ragged shirt and trousers gave me the impression he must be some kind of gardener or retainer. He pulled a key from his pocket and unlocked the front door, went into the house and came back three or four minutes later with at least two bottles of wine in his arms and what looked like a number of groceries. These he put in the back of the Fiat, relocked the front door and got in and drove off. I couldn't resist a slight smile; the owner whoever he was, was being quietly robbed on one hand and was about to be quietly ditto on the other, that is if he had anything to suit my book.

The seclusion of this villa, from my point of view, was near perfect. The drive, after it left the house by some fifty yards, turned round a corner and disappeared. I let matters drift until about seven, then got up and put the bits and pieces back in the car. When I had locked it I walked away and round in an arc that was intended to bring me into a little olive grove at the back of my target. After about ten minutes walking and scrambling, it did.

The first thing I now did was to dodge around a bit to

down where the drive went round the corner. When I got there I saw that it wound its way down for about half a mile, and the entrance gate seemed to be by a stone single-storey house. It was presumably the place where the light-fingered retainer had come from. I gave it a search over with the glasses and saw nothing more than a plume of smoke coming from the chimney. I imagined they were getting down to a feast on their boss's account.

I retraced my steps to the back of the villa. Here I examined the windows and door. The latter seemed well secured. I turned my attention to the window on the right-hand side of the door. With my knife I was able to work away at the latch until it lifted up and the window was open. I climbed in, then carefully dusted away the small chips of paint that had come off with the action of the knife, after which I pulled the window to and relatched it. I went through the house first at a fast trot. If only I had found this earlier I would not have had all that bother north of Venice. The owner of this place had taste and funds. There were fine examples of late fifteenth- and sixteenth-century work not only from Italy, but also from the Flemish and early German Schools. It was going to be one of those times when I have to contain my appetite. I felt I wanted to back up a lorry and take the lot.

I gathered myself together, took a good look round and selected a fine 'Allegory on the garden of Eden', which was on copper, and which looked as though it were by Jan 'Velvet' Brueghel; the figures were so luscious that they might even have been put in by Rubens. On the opposite wall I chose an 'Entombment', and this, to my eye, gave every evidence that it was either by Hans Memling or very close indeed. This was on a wooden panel. In the hall I found the third one to complete my list. It was a quite exquisite 'Adoration of the Kings' which looked as if it could be by the hand of Pieter Brueghel the Elder. All three of these were conveniently small. In the kitchen I found some cord and paper and bundled them together.

Out of the window, and with a little fiddling I managed to get the latch to fall back into place. I retraced my steps through the olive grove and round to the car and by nine I was on the road again. Now, however, I turned to the right when I got down to Bologna, instead of continuing to the south. Just before Modena I found a bed for the night. The next morning I drove on through Parma and then filtered over and through the mountains by Pornovo di Taro and Pontremoli and rejoined the west coast road close to Spezia. So up towards Genoa and the frontier. During the last few days I had kept aware of the news but had heard or read nothing to indicate a major scare from the districts I had been operating in.

As soon as I was over the frontier I stopped for the night and for a mild celebration dinner. The next day I made my way to Paris to make arrangements with my restorer friend to reline the five that I had sandwiched. He said it would take until early September.

Thence back to the French house. It was now a matter of containing myself for a period. I worked out a few routes for the coming trip. I also made out a list of dealers to visit. Whatever I did was going to be pretty much in the dark. The route I thought would be the best, when I saw the dealer's addresses, was Burgos, Salamanca, Seville, Cordoba and Madrid. If this little lot produced nothing, there were some possibles in Zaragoza, Barcelona and Valencia.

By September 10 I had the pictures back from Paris. I had now to do a little work on them myself. I had had to get the reline done in France because if I had arrived in Spain with the sandwiches, any dealer was going to be suspicious. Therefore, I now had to disguise them again for the trip to Spain.

What I did was to stretch a piece of thin primed dark canvas over the front of the pictures and round on to the back of the stretchers, and staple this canvas into position so that it covered the edges of the reline canvas. To complete the look of the thing I ran a few staples round the edges of the stretchers. The copper panel I treated to my sandwich method. The other two Flemish pictures were on wooden panels and I couldn't do much more with these than wrap them in some soft cloth. When I loaded the car with my amateur artist's rig and the concocted canvases I found the panels would stow away out of sight between the canvases.

I had decided to enter Spain round the west end of the Pyrenees. Accordingly I drove across to Bordeaux and then down that almost endless flat dull road mostly through tall pine forests to Bayonne, Biarritz and so to the frontier.

No bother. the briefest examination of passport, insurance documents, a thump of a rubber stamp. The most civil and polite wave through.

I carried on along the coast road till I got to San Sebastian and then turned away to the south going through Tolosa and on to Vitoria. Before dinner time I had made Burgos. I even found a small hotel that knew someone who had a lock-up garage. I was fortunate.

The next morning my attention did wander from the business side, because I just had to take the camera and work away for a time at the cathedral. This has an air of fantasy about it with its spires and asymmetric design viewed from outside. It was begun about 1221 and they did not get round to finishing it until 1567. In all it has fifteen chapels. Here is buried El Cid, a gentleman whom I think if I had met at a different place and a different time I could have had a great deal in common with.

During the afternoon and the following day I sought out the names that I had listed for Burgos. I drew a blank. Oh well, I had plenty of time in hand; even if I did run up a pretty expensive account.

The day after this fruitless search I set out for Salamanca. These plains of Spain have a weird quality. The road that went through Valladolid was nowhere what one could call very good. In many parts it was rather hump-backed, narrow and the verges were crumbling away. Fortunately the traffic was light. The scenery was mainly seemingly endless undulating low-hilled expanses of drought-dried grass. Trees, what there were of them, consisted of isolated gnarled old olives that at times seemed to be writhing for lack of moisture. Now and then there were groves of younger olives showing some signs of being tended. Occasionally vineyards had the vines crawling along the broken soil. There was the odd bird of prey hovering high and watchful in a cloudless sky. Every now and then a field with the inevitable black bulls.

Valladolid was a place that left little on the memory except that Columbus had died there in 1506 and it had been the home of the writer Cervantes. I only paused long enough for a drink and a snack.

In the afternoon I drove and drove across more and more Spanish plain. By about five I crossed the old bridge and drove up into the town of Salamanca. I found some lodgings as well as a place to lock the car up. After I had washed and tidied up a bit I went for a stroll through the great arcaded Plaza Mayor, and sat for a while with a glass of dry sherry and a small dish of olives.

The next day did bring a little light on the scene; for the third dealer I visited had something and he would trade. I found him in a street at the back of the Plaza Mayor. He was a pleasant fellow. I explained that like him I was in the 'trade' and looking out for pictures for a client in America who had given me some of his Italian and Flemish pictures with which he wished me if possible to make an arrangement, as he wanted to possess some Spanish paintings. My dealer couldn't have been more helpful. First of all he turned up a delightful flower painting by Juan de Arellano, who was born at Santorcaz in 1614 and had studied with Juan de Solis. The painting was quite exquisite, colouring faultless and so was the draughtsmanship. He next produced a portrait of a young man in a richly embroidered and tailored costume against an almost black background, the features well modelled. This was by Alonzo Sanchez Coello, who was one of the favourite painters of Philip II, who likened him to Titian.

I was more than pleased with these two and went back to the car to fetch my wares. When I unpacked them I could see at once from his reactions that I had guessed right. He said, "Let us put the Jan Brueghel beside the Coello. I think there is a good match. What do you think?"

I agreed quite readily, as only he could lose after all. He then picked one of the smaller Madonnas and Child, as he said he had a ready customer for it. He thought it was a little better than the flower painting. Well, who was I to argue? To seal that bargain he most generously gave me a large sum of pesetas, which I worked out afterwards as being in the neighbourhood of £300.

I felt that Salamanca had done its stuff, so I did not linger there. I had an early and somewhat soporific night with an excellent bottle of wine, and by nine the next morning I was on the way to Seville, over three hundred miles away to the south. It was a city I had not visited before, and it was with genuine pleasure that I promised myself, come what may, at least two days plain tourism after the business.

Seville has another of these special cathedrals that seem indigenous to Spain, at least in part of their creation. It is fifteenth-/sixteenth-century Gothic and is one of the largest churches in the world. The campanile is of Moorish origin, the Giralda, some 300 feet high. Seville, too, I knew claimed some of its fame from being the birthplace of two of Spain's leading painters: Velazquez and Murillo.

The dealers of this city also were very co-operative. In fact, apart from finding a still life, I made a clean sweep and got the five other portraits. First was 'Don Juan of Austria' by Eugenio de las Cuevas, who was appointed by Philip IV to instruct his son the said Don Juan. The same dealer also produced 'Philip III' by Juan de la Corte, born in Madrid in 1597, who had been taught by Velazquez. Then from another visit came 'Isabel of Valois', the third wife of Philip II, which was by Juan Pantoja de la Cruz, born in 1551, who had studied with Sanchez Coello. He was noticed by Philip II who named him as one of his painters and valets-de-chambre. The next was by Blas del Prado. He was born somewhere near Toledo about 1540 and studied with Alonso Berruguete. This turned out to be a study of one of the Princesses of the Harem which he had painted when on a visit to the court of the Emperor of Morocco. The last one, royal again; but this time a portrait of Philip IV by Juan Bautista Martinez del Mazo. I had come across him in my discussion with André, and knew he was a very qualified copyist as well as a versatile painter.

At the end of all this I was left with just the 'Adoration of the Kings' – by Pieter Brueghel the Elder or near miss – to barter for a still life. Moreover the business had been done so quickly that I was able to have my days of sight-seeing. I changed my plans slightly and left one day earlier for Cordoba. Dealer, contact-wise, like Burgos, was a blank. So on to Madrid.

The second individual I called on had a quite likeable still life by Pedro de Castro, a painter of some skill, although very little is known about his life; he is thought, however, to have died in 1663. This particular picture was most skilfully arranged with carefully calculated colour harmonies and positively brilliant use of light and shade. I produced the 'Adoration' and the dealer went into almost embarrassing raptures over it. Little more need be said other than half an hour later I emerged with two good glasses of dry sherry inside me and another wad of pesetas, which this time added up to about £400.

Well, here I was near the end of September and jumping the gun by three months. I found myself a pleasant hotel, plus garage. Having deposited my luggage, I had a shower and changed. I then went out into the street and walked along for about a quarter of a mile at which point I decided to step into one of the other hotels and have some drinks and then a meal. I also decided to ask the telephone girl if she could put through a call to the States for me. When she acquiesced I gave her Robert's number. I reckoned this way I should catch him at his lunch, and sure enough I did. He went off like a young schoolboy who had been promised an extra week's holiday, saying, "Oh, I am glad. It isn't possible. It's marvellous. No, you're not too soon. Do you know, I've been promising myself a visit to Spain because there's some horse-flesh I want to see."

For him he was quite discreet. I had just said I had his order complete. He went on to tell me that he would hop a plane, and would be with me in a week. I asked him where he would be staying when he was in Madrid and he gave me the name of the hotel. There and then he made a date to meet me for lunch in exactly seven days' time. If he couldn't make it he'd get in touch with me at my hotel, the name of which I had given him.

There was no snag and at half past twelve on the day chosen I arrived, plus slightly bulky package, at his hotel. This time I had the pictures looking reasonably smart in a new green canvas grip. The porter directed me to Robert's room. I had scarcely knocked on the door before he was wringing my hand. Within five minutes he had relieved me of the grip, unzipped it and unpacked the pictures. He commenced to put them in a row round his room. He had forgotten to lock the door on this occasion, so I did it for him. Robert stopped half-way round and motioned to the drinks on the table, for me to help myself and him. Today he said he was on Scotch. I stayed on the wine of the country. He went on round the circuit, and then the questions started, for this was new ground for him. He didn't know the work of any of the painters; he had just about heard of Coello, and that was it.

I started to fill him in with provenances and all the details I could. I felt all was going well until we arrived at the 'Princess in the Harem'. I put across the story about the Emperor of Morocco, the Moors, Spain, and I almost turned it into a travelogue. I need not have bothered. He was staring at it, fascinated.

"Charles, that's a little beauty. Just look at how he's got that girl's face. The eyes. Oh gee . . . I'm goin' to go and sit in this room of my wife's many times and look at this girl – she's a real beauty."

I breathed a large sigh of relief and we ended up with the flower-piece and the still life. Again I had a very satisfied customer. What I didn't realize was, that I was entering, in fact, I was already in, that very strange area of relationship of the collector and his dealer.

Robert asked me what he owed me for the eight paintings. I told him a quite healthy sum, comfortably into five figures. As before, he was most generous and made it up with a thousand pounds for expenses. There on the table was the black brief-case with the brass lock. Sure enough, in a minute I was standing with a large fat handful of hundred dollar bills. On this occasion I was more ready for it, as light-weight suiting is no place to stuff that kind of money; I had brought with me, in the canvas grip, a small brief-case in which I could stow the loot. I asked him if he would like me to help in any way with the packing or onward routing. He told me I need not worry over these problems. All would be taken care of, as one of his friends freighters was going to pick up what was wanted from Bilboa.

"Now, Charles, what are your moves, that is, after I have given you a real good lunch?"

I thanked him regarding the lunch and told him that as I had some fairly urgent business in France, I should have to be off soon afterwards. He continued, "Well, that's all right by me, Charles, but look you here, don't go leaving me several years like this again. Tell you what, my friend, you just give me a call about every six months, because I think we have a lot more business to get through."

It was an excellent lunch. When we parted Robert came to the foyer and saw me off with the warmest of hand-shakes. On leaving him, I went down the street to the nearest money-changer and shifted a few of those dollars into pesetas. I intended to spoil myself a little on the way. I spent eight days very pleasantly. I called in at Valencia, which was hardly on my direct route to France. This was followed by Barcelona, Zaragoza, Pamplona, and then back through San Sebastian, over the frontier for two days of luxury in Biarritz.

* * *

In April of 1959 I found that the little French house was

beginning to get clogged with the amount of reference material I had accrued over the years. Added to this, rooms were also getting over-filled because I had been visiting sales and picking up interesting pieces of furniture that pleased me. I decided that my changing circumstances were calling for somewhere with more space and perhaps more elegance. At the moment I had no idea where this might be. On recent trips to London I had taken to travelling via Ostend for some unaccountable reason, and on landing back there had thought it could be a much better starting point for reaching out into the various corners of Europe. It was easy to get to Holland, Germany, even up into Denmark. The roads were more direct down to Switzerland and Italy, and it was, of course, equally available for France. So I thought possibly when I did find the right place to expand in it mightn't be a bad idea if it were within, say, twelve hours' drive from Ostend.

In June I had an enjoyable reunion with Robert whom I had rung up in May. He came over with bulging brief-case but this time mostly crammed with photographs of his family, house, paddocks and stables. At his request, for three days I walked him round the galleries in Holland: the Boymans in Rotterdam, the Rijksmuseum, and certainly one of my favourites, the Mauritshuis in The Hague. For one frightening moment, I thought he was going to go all over Rembrandt and Hals and build himself another room, giving me an order for twelve. But he didn't. Instead he left me with quite a simple list, for him. We were back on the sporting pictures — "Another six, please Charles." Thank goodness, there was no immediate hurry.

*　　*　　*

It was August, one of those days when one feels full of joy. I went into a dealer's show-room in Brussels and could hear he was in a confab in his inner office, somewhat ill-advisedly having shut his door. It must have been some very secretive business. As I was looking round I spotted a very fine Sienese 'Madonna and Child' hung hidden away in a dark corner. I recognized the panel because I had been told about it and shown a photograph some three years earlier, when it had been stolen. There was a small framed portrait of a girl, almost the same size as the Madonna, leaning against the wall. Without hesitation, I took a quick squint behind the Madonna – all was well – and lifted her off the wall. Hung the girl's portrait in its place, and sauntered out of the show-room, just carrying the picture nonchalantly. I have found this open innocent manner often works. Twenty yards down the street a Belgian policeman wished me good morning. I seemed to attract about as much notice as if I were carrying a tray of loaves. I turned off to the right to where my car was parked, put the painting in the back, threw a rug over it, and, as it was such a fine day, drove straight down to Alsace.

By nine o'clock that evening my usual 'friend' there had bought it. He was really becoming friendly. I had whistled several pieces along to him during the years, and I think he now began to regard me as some sort of cog-wheel in his supply line, and therefore to be treated, as he saw it, fairly.

But my mind was also on other things, as I motored round on business or pleasure, I was keeping my eyes skinned for that likely place I needed. I wasn't sure whether it would be best to be in a town, a village or out in the country. They all had advantages and disadvantages. I knocked out the village idea, because if it were small, nothing but nothing was going to be secret. My little place in Italy was quite different, but this would be my main establishment, anyway for the foreseeable future. And although I naturally keep things as close as I can, I didn't want any unnecessary leaks.

*   *   *

By about mid-March 1960 I had managed to collect the next bunch for Robert. Four of them I had picked up in Holland, a somewhat unlikely place for pictures by Alken & Co.; and the other two I had managed to get from a very carelessly tended house in the Cambridge area. I had to ring Robert several times before I got him, as apparently he was away travelling. When I did contact him early in April, sure enough he hopped a plane. These well-lined Americans think about as little of getting on a plane as we Europeans think of taking a bus.

I met him in Holland at Schiphol airport some five miles out from Amsterdam. He scanned the canvases through and again was delighted. Out came that black brief-case. For getting them back to the States, there would, of course, be one of his friend's freighters coming along to Rotterdam. I never found out how many ships this friend owned but they always seemed to be hovering ready.

I was determined now to get a move on in my search for the new house. For the whole of the summer and much of the autumn of 1960 I was roving far and wide within my given radius from Ostend. There were so many dead-ends, so many places that appeared just right and then the snags followed. I started to feel a bit desperate, which is always a dangerous thing to do. Ultimately, in late September, the number did come up. I found it.

A large estate was having a bit of a split-up. Parcels of land and cottages were being sold to tenant farmers and a number of houses were on offer. It was pleasant country, reasonably high above sea-level. The scenery was not dramatic; it was undemanding, peaceful. The part of the property that I clicked on almost as soon as I saw it was a house built somewhere about 1700 to 1720. It was in the stone of the area with a mixed roofing of slates and tiles that had been done at different periods. It stood on a small spur of land in a loop of the little river that ran through the estate. It was well-nigh like being on a tiny island, because the river cut back on itself so much that the neck of land was only a few yards wider than the narrow road which came off the main estate drive. This approach ended up in a walled court-yard at the side of the house.

There were four bedrooms and one rather dilapidated bathroom. On the ground-floor there was a large drawing-room with a fine marble fire-place, and behind this a small but large enough dining-room, which sided on to the kitchen. The other side of the hall there was a room that must have been used for games; billiards, ping-pong and the like. In the court-yard were a garage large enough for two cars and what appeared to have been stables but these had been turned into a workshop.

The small piece of land in front of it had at one time been a terraced garden which had now fallen sadly into neglect.

I went over the place very thoroughly and from what knowledge I had, it seemed structurally sound, although it was going to need a great deal of restoring. After two hours I went up to see the owner of the estate, who was elderly, tall and angular, and his wife. At first they greeted me coolly. I realized that they were now doing the inspecting; wondering what I would be like to have as a not-so-distant neighbour. Their reactions must have proved favourable; for after about fifteen minutes his wife rang a bell and when a maid appeared she asked for drinks to be brought in.

The price that they were asking was fairly steep; but then it really was what I wanted, and I didn't quibble. The legal matters took about three months to go through, as these things are wont to do. But by the first week in January 1961 I had the deeds and was the new owner. It was rather an odd experience I found because with that house I saw somewhere that I could really love; where I could put roots down. I shut out of my mind other thoughts that are associated with roots going down, and threw myself into the task of getting my house exactly the way I wanted it. This meant plenty of driving backwards and forwards until April. By then the builders and decorators had completed enough for me to move in.

The little house with the stone wall and the railings and with the grain store next to it sold quite quickly. I did feel a few pangs as I left it.

The furniture that I had there seemed small and inadequate in the new place. But the bulk of cartons and cases with books, files and research material overflowed the games-room, which was to be the study. I sequestered one of the bedrooms as a store.

During the summer I watched the house and the garden grow. I had found a man who worked on the estate who was prepared to come in evenings and week-ends to work on the terrace. Already with his skilled hands tidiness was emerging and flowers were blooming. He consulted me as to what I wanted to do with quite a large piece that had been left as grass at the side of the house where the court-yard was. Between us we decided to have a small orchard planted there. He had also found me the wife of a friend who would come in when I wanted her to clean and polish; she also did my laundry and mending.

By the autumn the last of the builders moved out. The house had been rewired and the decoration was complete. There had been one other matter for which I had engaged a specialist firm to come down on two consecutive week-ends.

I was having a wall-safe put in; this was primarily for my index-books and also to hold the sometimes bulky wads of notes I accumulate before running them to the bank in Switzerland.

My interview with the security firm whom I was engaging to do the work enlightened me somewhat as to what equipment could be available. The sales manager reeled off a series of devices to defeat a thief, which included; a gadget which released jets of steam when the combination knob was used wrongly; a stiletto blade which sprang out – and he could also arrange for a built-in gun; and what I thought was a real science-fiction thing, a pair of metal pincers which would jump out and clamp on to one's hands. Every time I get near a safe after this informative meeting my stomach tends to knot up somewhat inside.

The safe I selected for myself was a three-ring combination, which with its multiples of numbers gives an odds of one million to one. The place I chose for it was in the wall behind two of my large filing-cabinets; these the men bolted together and then mounted them on a set of special low casters. From outward appearances they looked the same. The thick carpet came right up to them and disguised the very small gain in height from the casters. If the carpet were turned back the cabinets could easily be pulled away from the wall.

After the job was finished I found myself playing with the combination until I found I had it taped. I did even go so far as to buy a stethoscope and become reasonably proficient with hearing the workings moving about as the knob was turned. I worked at it in daylight, in the dusk, by torch-light and in complete darkness. On several occasions in the future this was to prove to have been useful practice.

I returned to my visiting of sales and would frequently come back with the car piled with carpets or odd pieces of furniture. If my daily happened to be there she would greet these with approving noises.

Christmas that year I spent in solitary but not lonely contentment. The fire-place in the drawing-room allowed for the type of log-fire I could remember from my boyhood in Cornwall. My help – I found out the day before Christmas – had spent nearly the whole day baking and getting things ready for me, so that, as she put it, I would not be hungry over the Season. When she had gone I went into the larder and it was stacked with cooked fruits, savoury meats, and gay little cakes.

Christmas Eve was dry and frosty. In the evening the sky overhead was pricked out with uncountable numbers of stars. I put on a sheepskin coat and walked down the road to the main drive and into the village which was about a mile and a half away. I felt a sensation I hadn't really known for a long, long time; there seemed a oneness with what was going on. I wasn't, for the moment, the stranger outside any more. I went into one of the taverns which was heady with tobacco smoke, beer and strong drink. I found a place for myself and sat long over two drinks, secure in this throng.

After an hour I went out into the street and saw a steady stream of people of all ages moving down towards the church that stood with its windows sparkling colours from the lights inside.

*   *   *

In April 1962 I decided to dispense with the small Italian flat. By then I had changed to a Citroën Safari and I set off in this to arrange matters with the priest. I sold most of the sticks of furniture and what bits I wanted to keep I put in the back of the Estate for the journey home.

The bi-annual phone call in June to Robert didn't

produce any orders, but again he was pestering me to come over to the States. I felt that I really must make plans to go over and see him and America. After all, ever since the forays of Duveen, this had been where some of the biggest buyers of all time had come from. And it was where a fairly large proportion of the world's art gravitated to. I wasn't quite sure what plan of action I would operate on over there or what type or merchandise I would take with me. I didn't really see the feasibility of arriving with a large stock of bulky paintings. I felt there could be a better course with less risks. Although it was a long way ahead, the spring of 1964 would be a good target date.

In the late autumn I went over to London for a go round the galleries and sale-rooms; foraging more for information than for actual objects. I was interested to see how the various categories of antiques and fine art objects were starting to climb in value with a steady momentum. The vagaries of prices always rather intrigue me. With some painters like Rembrandt and Dürer, it is a straight forward upward line. Yet with others like Teniers or Corot, the price line goes up and down. Corot had his peak in the late nineteenth century and the early years of this. Today he has dropped back. Teniers had his high in the late eighteenth century, fell down in 1930 and is now rising again.

With the works of some artists it is difficult to see just why there are these price variations. It can't all be satisfactorily explained away by fashion. It is equally difficult to forecast when one of these up and down tangles is coming.

There was one category struck me especially; prints, such as etchings, woodcuts, wood engravings and metal engravings of master quality. They were responding in a healthy way. Then I had it. Here could be an ideal solution for the American trip. I would spend time in the interval putting together a really outstanding folio for my hoped for customers over there. Several hundred prints would take up very little room and could no doubt be convincingly disguised.

When I was back in the house over the Channel I dug deep into the whereabouts book and managed to get a fair idea of the areas I must search to find what I was after. I pinpointed them on a map and worked out my campaign. For most of 1963 it was fairly hard going and I didn't see a great deal of my home. But after trips down to Bavaria, the neighbourhood of Cologne, Holland, Rome, Switzerland, Luxembourg, and a rather hectic ten days rustling round Britain, I did have what I wanted. Indeed, matters had rather taken things into their own hands and I had more than what I had set out to get, because with a number of the folios, cabinets and walls I had rifled, frequently in close proximity to the prints would be drawings, water colours, works in gouache or pen and ink which were really too tempting. In retrospect, I can recall the frame-disposal question from this lot had been quite a problem in itself.

I spent the next two months happily engaged in sorting out the collection. The preparation of a well-ordered catalogue does take a time, and in the heat of the moment on several occasions I hadn't, with this garnering, had the minutes to spare to make sure exactly what I was getting. So I was really pleased when out of some four hundred and forty-two examples of the kind of things I've mentioned there were only three which I put under the heading of poor and not worth taking.

Early in December I gave Robert his statutory call. I had told him the previous June that I was planning to come over in March or April 1964 and he had got it all worked out. His shopping list this time was just one item. However, from him the subject was a surprise to me. He said:

"Charles, I want one of those early Flemish religious

paintings. I don't mind really who it is by as long as it's good. I don't want any of these Crucifixions or Entombments. I want an Adoration of the Kings or Magi or Shepherds ... a Nativity or Annunciation. Some subject like that. Can you do it for me?" Then without waiting for a reply, he charged on: "Now when you come over Charles, I expect you're going to aim to bring what you call stock with you. Now, I've explained to you that these things can be different comin' in our end. I'm wondering if I can be any help to you. Now don't go thinking in terms of bringing in Michelangelo's David or the Mona Lisa or anything like that," and he gave a hearty laugh. Then I learnt as he went on that what he was offering, bless his generous heart, was that anything I had for myself to dispose of I should wrap up with the picture I had on order from him. He said that if I rang him mid-February he would have it all hunky-dory. He'd give me the name of the freighter belonging to that friend, and all the details of whom to go to and ask for, where she'd be, and how to do everything. This was quite a load off my mind, because with the batch of stuff that I was aiming to take, it could have been a problem. I suppose there might have been an amateur disguise such as a large atlas, but I think this could have been a risky one for several reasons.

Immediately after Christmas I got on to the travel people and booked myself first-class on one of the smaller Cunarders, leaving March or April. I then had to get this visa business sorted out which America insists all us aliens have to have when we go over there. The form was lengthy and asked many questions, but after a couple of hours 'watch-and-care' work I had it made out looking fairly innocent. It must have been thought acceptable because by mid-February I had my visa.

Meanwhile I had the problem of Robert's last order. I

knew he wanted quality, top-grade this time, and paintings in this category by the early Flemish, Dutch or German painters aren't exactly the easiest things to come across in my mode of acquiring merchandise. It was no good doing the lift from a gallery even if I got away with it, because the type of picture I was after would carry a lot of publicity if it sailed out of a public collection, and it would be almost bound to be picked up by the States news-boys. Robert, I knew, looked on me as a straight guy, despite his what he thought witty crack about the Michelangelo and the Mona Lisa. I didn't want him disillusioned.

There was nothing for it but to go burrowing deep into my library, files and index-boxes to see if I could sort out a list of likely painters and then rake deep to find out where their paintings were or might be. It took me about five days, and then I felt I was on the way to getting matters started.

In transcripts of some Italian documents I came across a mention of a visiting Flemish painter, one Gheeraert David. He was, of course, the celebrated artist of the fifteenth century. Like many another painter he had, to a degree, been lost in history. Apparently his name was known to the writers Guicciardini and Sanderus. But it wasn't until after the middle of the nineteenth century that he became at all well documented. The archives of Bruges proved that this 'Gerard, son of John, son of David,' was a native of Oudewater in South Holland, and that he settled in Bruges in 1483, being admitted there in 1484 as a Master Painter into the Guild of St Luke. Clearly he was a man with a likeable nature and had an excellent reputation both as a painter and as a miniaturist. Who actually taught him is not quite plain, but it is possible that he was in the studio of Dirk Bouts for a time, although the richness of his colouring also suggests that he got this feature at any rate from

Italy. I found, too, that he had been in Florence and had been particularly impressed with the work of Carpaccio.

Something by David, I concluded, would be perfect, if I could track down an example which it might be possible for me to get hold of. David's manner has a combination of the mysticism of the Renaissance and the feeling conveyed by the early Flemish artists, with at times the jewel-like quality of the details found in the work of the Van Eycks. Subject matter, excellent. I noted everything about him that I could find. Sometimes I strained my language abilities to the limit, but I persevered, and then rather late one night, some hope came through.

There was a mention of a panel entitled 'The Blessed Virgin and Child Enthroned with Saints and Angels' that had been purchased by a certain Giulio Santi who seemed to have had some association with Francesco Maria della Rovere (who was left his coronet by Guidubaldo, the last Duke of Urbino in the Montefeltro line). Ploughing on, about two pages later there was a notation of how the purchaser had written a letter to an uncle saying how pleased he was with the panel of 'The Blessed Virgin and Child Enthroned with Saints and Angels' by this Flemish artist Gheeraert. Well, there was the picture, but where was it now?

Over the years I had been building up my research library, I had oftentimes wondered if perhaps I was pushing just a little too much money into the shelves. But when this kind of thing came through, it made the investment, which I think then totalled well over twenty thousand pounds, pay off.

I continued the chase. The next day I found that the picture had passed down through three generations of Giulio Santi's family and had then been sold to a scholar by the name of Martin Woermann in the late sixteenth century.

He had left it to his son, Hans, whose business as a minor architect failed shortly after his father's death. The Gheeraert David with most of Hans's other effects had been sold. The purchaser of the panel had been a merchant, Gunther Eberhard, and it had then remained in his family until early in the nineteenth century, when they had sold it. The buyer had been a citizen of Aachen, and then the trail went dead on me. Try as I might I could not pick it up. To have traced it through some four hundred odd years and then to lose it so near was maddening.

As a last resort I turned to the studio books of André. I started at the beginning and laboriously went through all his records of restoration work that he had done. Suddenly, in May 1932, there was the David again, fully listed. It had been brought to André by the gentleman from Aachen's, I suppose, great-great-great grandson. There were details of what had been necessary, how the panel had split and what treatment André had given it, and the retouching involved. Hopefully I went on through these books. Then in 1943 André had had the picture for treatment again, brought to him, it seemed, by a frau from the same family. There had been surface scratches in the bottom left-hand corner and some blistering towards the right-hand side close to the edge. So I had pinned it down to 1943 and as being in Aachen or that area.

I packed a grip with some clothes, a bag with a few essential tools and etceteras, and got out the car. It took me the best part of a day's drive to get to Aachen. When I arrived I booked into a small unremarkable hotel and started the search.

First of all I turned to the telephone directory and found that there were rather a lot of people with the name that I was after; but with the Christian name, it was narrowed down. I made a note of their addresses and began to feel my way through with surreptitious enquiries. After some time I did land on the one that I felt it must be. The others, by their jobs, addresses and other details that I had gleaned, appeared unlikely.

My suspect was elderly and lived the life of a recluse a few kilometres out of Aachen. A visit to the back editions library of a newspaper office gave me some enlightening information; it was from those papers that were immediately after the war and the re-establishment of the administration in Aachen. In these I came across some small snippets which gave a lead to the fellow I was intending to visit. He had more than blotted his book. He was not so much a recluse as an outcast.

It was by then late in the day and I decided that matters must wait.

At four o'clock the next afternoon, whilst there was still light, I drove out to the district and found his house. I took the car about a quarter of a mile away and parked down a convenient cul-de-sac, which seemed only to lead to a deserted building-material store.

By seven o'clock it was good and dark. Taking a torch, a pair of gloves, my knife and the odd tools, I walked back towards the house and slipped into the garden through a small wicket. This had been a bit of a mistake as I had got tangled up with a mass of fruit bushes and then staggered into some heavy evergreens. But I got clear and walked across a small lawn and then on to the tarmac drive.

There was one light visible in the bay-window of the room to the left of the front door. I tried to find a space in the curtaining across the front of the bay to peer through, but there was none. I edged my way round to the right of the bay-window and tried again there. Better luck. Where the curtains had been pulled a little too far across was an adequate gap at the side. From there I could see into the room but only in a rather restricted manner, until I spotted a very large gilt framed mirror over the fire-place in the wall facing me. Studying this, I found that I could take in a large part of the room indirectly.

There was my man, sitting at a table on which appeared to be the remains of a supper left for him no doubt by his housekeeper or somesuch. I couldn't make out what he was eating as he had his back to the fire-place and the mirror. I could see a bottle of corn spirit and a glass to his right, and as I watched he drained the glass and poured another three-finger helping. After a few minutes he pushed away his empty plate and pulled over a loaf of dark brown bread on a board, cut a slice and then made a long arm for the cheese. During the eating of this he again drained his glass, and picked up the bottle and appeared to study the contents for a moment. I thought he must be working out whether or not he had had his ration; evidently not quite, for he poured out another inch. When he finished the cheese he gulped the drink down and got up.

Not a pretty person; a short bent figure, a large round head, with the eyes deep-sunken, so that with the overhead light their sockets looked more like thumb-sized holes. He was almost totally bald with just a few straggling greasy grey locks draped over his collar, the top of his head disfigured with king-sized brown blotches.

He went round, limping heavily, to a small desk against the wall opposite the mirror and behind the table. He must have been then only about ten feet away from me to the right.

Reaching up, he lifted a picture of a dark lady from the wall and disclosed a large wall-safe. Having lent the picture against the side of the desk, he felt in a waistcoat pocket and must have pulled out a key, for I saw him fiddling with one of the drawers of the desk and then pull it open. He lifted something out which when he held it up to the light I could make out was a small note-book. He must have found the page he was looking for as he then put the note-book in his left hand and started to dial the combination numbers of the safe. After he had finished this he moved the lever grip and the door came open. He put the note-book back in the drawer and locked it, putting the key back in his waistcoat pocket. I couldn't make out clearly what was in the safe. But there did appear to be a tall bundle on the left-hand side. Some insight seemed to point to this. I felt it would be quite on the slate for a character like this to keep what I was after locked away.

He turned round, crossed the room until he was out of sight, then reappeared carrying a cardboard shoebox. He put it down on the top of the desk, lifted the lid and took out something wrapped in dark tissue paper. The spindly hands took this off to show a fine two-armed silver candlestick, which by its decoration must have been around 1770 for date. After an admiring glance he placed the candlestick in the safe, shut the door and scrambled the combination; lastly he rehung the portrait over the safe.

He then came back to the table and reached over to pick up a bottle which seemed to have a chemist's prescription label on it. From this he tipped out two white tablets on to the polished surface of the table. He poured a glass of mineral water and swallowed both of them. I could only imagine that these were some sort of sleeping pills because immediately after he had taken them, he shuffled to the door, put out the light and tramped away out of my sight into the hall. Almost at once I noticed a light come on in an upstairs window, I presumed on a landing. I thought to myself that if those were sleeping pills they should combine with the rough spirit to put him well and truly in the 'far away' within fairly quick time.

I went back a few paces from the house and walked round it slowly to see if I could get the geography of what was happening. Four more lights were now showing from behind curtains, and I could only surmise that they must represent his bedroom, bathroom and possibly a dressing-room. I drew back towards a small shed which would give a little shelter from the cold wind that was getting up. After ten minutes the right-hand light had gone out, followed about three minutes later by the next one to it; then what I had thought was the landing light. The remaining two stayed on I suppose for another quarter of an hour, after which it was all dark.

By now it was something after eight and I had to work out how long I was going to wait before going in. Caution said give it three hours. The cold that was already nasty said an hour and a half. I recall thinking to myself, well, this is what you have been training yourself to do all along; so let's see what you can do. Somehow I got through the hour and a half and then went to it.

I walked across to the bay-window through which I had been watching; and pulled on my gloves, I examined the centre frames with the merest glimmer from my torch. There was a hefty screw safety-bolt in the secure position.

This time Mr Hood was going to have to use a trick or two from one of those crooked manuals he had studied. Fortunately this window must be about as far from the inhabitant's bedroom as possible, which was a plus point.

I had practised this glass-cutting lark a number of times in the daylight back at the house and it all seemed very simple. But it was not so on a strange window and in the dark, and well chilled.

Shielding the torch-light to almost nothing inside my closed fingers, I pulled a diamond-tipped glass-cutter out of a jacket pocket and applied it to the pane just above the safety-bolt. In my eagerness I must have almost pushed the cutter through the glass, for there was a deep graze marking off the oblong patch which I had worked on. Next I stuck a length of sticky tape across the patch and then got out a small rubber sucker on a wooden handle. I gave this a good lick and gently pressed it into the middle of the patch. Following this I wrapped a handkerchief round the fingers of my right hand. Then holding the handle of the rubber sucker and the torch with my left hand, I gave a sharpish knock with my right forefinger knuckle to one side of the patch. Nothing happened. I waited, catching my breath. Not a sound. It took me unpleasantly back to an incident in the war when I had had to use a hammer to free the keep ring round the fuse of a bomb the Germans didn't want made safe.

After two or three minutes I tried again and then another wait. It took three more of these nerve-paralysing moments before there came a dry crack and the patch came loose and went inwards to be held by the sucker and the tape. The latter I pulled off and then managed to work the sucker and the patch back through the oblong hole after a little twisting around.

The safety-bolt was soon unscrewed and I lifted it out of its catch; the window-fastening was undone; window open and I was in. Pause for a good long listen. Nothing. So across to door, another listen. Nothing. Then I pulled the curtains firmly across and put the small torch down on the desk underneath where the safe was. I lifted down the picture and lent it against the side of the desk. I took out a small bunch of skeleton keys. It was only a very simple cabinet lock in the drawer and the ninth one I tried turned it easily. Taking out the man's note-book, I turned the pages till I came across those vital figures for the combination. I was very grateful to him, as I didn't see myself in the role of some mechanical doctor with stethoscope in ears listening for the movements from the combination as I twiddled round the knob. This particular lock was very similar to the one on my own safe, which meant that it would have three rings which could give one million combinations of numbers. I think I would have had to have given it best.

Concentrating hard, I recalled the routine. The first number was 12, so round I spun the knob counterclockwise four times and stopped with the 12 opposite the arrow. The next was 82; this time I spun the knob clockwise three times and stopped with the 82 against the arrow; the last number was 23, round goes the knob counterclockwise twice again and 23 was opposite the arrow. Move the lever and open, sweet as summer, comes the door.

I pulled out his candlestick and several expensive looking leather cases which I presumed held jewellery.

I hoped I had guessed right. I felt I must have done. For there leaning against the left-hand side was this flat cloth-wrapped bundle. I pulled it out, slipped the bow of a tape securing it. Gheeraert had surfaced for me. I retied the bow. I was just about to put back the leather cases when I felt I must look inside them. The first one had a triple string of pearls. Right out of my depth. The second one had ear-rings, bracelet and pendant, again pearls. The third and last one – pearls again. I didn't know what my man was up to; but I thought I'd leave him to it. So back the boxes went in the safe plus the candlestick. I must be getting more selective. I had the feeling that the one upstairs could be a nutcase or a receiver of some kind. All the better. The door of the safe closed and I spun the knob to scramble things.

I picked up the portrait and was just about to hang it up again when the subdued gleam from the torch caught it. It looked interesting and then I held it closer to the light. There was a title plate which read: 'Infanta Clara Eugenia'. At that moment I couldn't imagine who it was by or even stop to look at all closely, but I suddenly had the idea it would be a nice little gesture to give Mrs Robert one for her collection. Give I felt, because Robert himself was going to have to pay plenty for the Gheeraert David. So, without more ado, I pulled up the nails securing it to the frame with a pair of pliers, lifted it out and with both the paintings under my arm I retreated in good order across the room and out of the window. I did close it behind me, although the man was going to have little in the way of doubts when he came to in the morning as to what had happened. If he was what I thought he was there wasn't going to be much he could do about it either, except curse.

The next morning I drove out into the country to examine the catch. The David, of course, was not framed. It was a beauty. It had all the qualities I had thought it would have plus that innate atmosphere of naïve sincerity which some of the painters at that time could evoke.

I looked at the portrait of the Infanta and was fascinated to see that I had picked quite a rarity. There was a label on the back with some details. It had been painted by Sofonisba Anguisciola. She had been born in Cremona about 1535. There had been six sisters, all of whom had painted: Elena, Lucia, Minerva, Europa, Anna Maria, and, of course, Sofonisba who had studied with Campi and Gatti, and had also lived and worked for some time in Spain. She had been in good favour with Philip II and had even been raised to the rank of first lady-in-waiting to the Infanta. It was an experience to have got hold of a painting by her, because in my book of painters' signatures I had, some time ago, noted down hers, 'Sofonisba Gentisdona Cremonese'.

When I got these two home I set about making a suitable packing-case to protect in particular the David panel on its long journey. I might have trusted the owners to whomever Robert gave them to for packing, but the David was a special commodity. The workshop had been refitted out in the court-yard and I quite enjoyed the job. The oak panel seemed to be in a good state despite its incarceration in the confines of the safe. The repairs to the split that André had done so long ago were holding well.

The case I made had allowances for controlling as far as possible the relative humidity and temperature. I hoped I had taken sufficient precautions to protect the picture from any knocks or bumps. I had also made enough room to put in the 'Infanta' and my bulky collection of prints and drawings. The David I had fitted into some blocks of plastic foam and then guided it into two channels so that it would be held upright, gently but firmly, with the paint surface well away from anything that might damage it. The materials that controlled the humidity were in four con-tainers, two at the bottom and two at the top. The whole case was lined inside with the foam material. When I finally screwed the lid on I felt it should keep a pretty even atmosphere for the trip.

In the middle of February I rang Robert. I didn't tell him about the 'Infanta', as I wanted it to be a surprise. I told him I had obtained a picture such as he wanted – I didn't tell him who it was by, for the same reason as before. But I did tell him I thought he would be satisfied. I stressed that when the case arrived he should not on any account open it before I got there because it had some special packing which I should like to unpack myself to be sure it was done safely. He promised to do as I asked, and then gave me my instructions. I was to have the case at Marseilles in about ten days' time. To drive up to such and such dock entrance. Park and go into the docks and find a ship, and he gave me the name. Ask for the captain, and he gave me the name; he would arrange the rest. "Then, Charles, just go back to your car and wait till they fetch the case," he had said.

Well, all this I did, and it seemed to work very smoothly.

* * *

By now the time was approaching for the boat-trip across. I packed my luggage, locked up the house, put the car in the garage, locked that up, and had a taxi take me to the station for the longish journey to Ostend. From there it was over to Dover and up to Liverpool to board the Cunarder.

In 1964 First Class Cunard across the Atlantic really meant something. My steward treated me with the feeling that he had been looking after me for years. The breakfast menu the first morning out sent one back glimpsing an already rare view of a world which was in all probability going to pass away for keeps. If I wanted to, I could wade through goodness knows what. But it was when I came to the main meals, the lunches and the dinners, that the luxury showed. The food from the Caviar Glacé through the Primeurs à la Grecque, the Turtle Soup au Xeres, the Scallopini Imbotti to the Strawberries Romanoff, plus the wine-list, plus the coffee and the liqueurs made me glad, but only for my waist-line's sake, that the trip lasted just about a week.

In a stabilized blood-mare such as this, the journey across the Pond was nothing but sheer joy, rest and peace. On the morning of our arrival, when the coast was still just a blur away on the western horizon, I found myself in a state of what I can only describe as schoolboy excitement. I had never been to America before. The ship was already beginning to slow down as we neared the coast. Not very long afterwards I could make out the Statue of Liberty and then, as we passed it, the Manhattan skyline was ahead reaching up to the clouds.

The ship had been docked, I had got clear of the immigration people and the customs, and now I was on the lookout for Robert. He had said he was going to drive up and meet the boat. Sure enough, there he was waving away like a windmill.

He really turned on the American hospitality. We went to a downtown restaurant, and after I had got over the shock of the size of the steak we settled in with both trying to talk the other down. Yes, the case had arrived about twelve days previous and he had locked it up in a lumber room because otherwise he just wouldn't have been able to keep his hands off it.

Later that afternoon we drove down towards the south. He decided he wasn't going to overdo it and we spent the night in Washington. The next morning we drove on for most of the day, and finally arrived at Robert's place about six. He introduced me to his wife. She was nearly as tall as he, slim and dark with olive skin. But most of all it was her eyes that betrayed her ancestry, dark crystals that lit up when she spoke and welcomed me.

Robert got out his keys and told me to follow him. He went through to the lumber-room and between the two of us we humped the case out into the hall. He found some tools, handed them to me and I undid the lid and very carefully lifted out the plastic foam packing on the top; then pulled out the David. I leant it against a wall that had a good strong side-light which brought it up to perfection. For a moment Robert was knocked absolutely silent. His wife stood beside him clutching her hands tightly. Robert spoke first: "Oh – I never would have guessed that I could have the chance to own something like this." For the moment that was all he said.

I fished out the sheet I had typed for him of the provenance, and he sat down and devoured it with glistening eyes. While he was going through it with his wife, I took out the portrait of the 'Infanta' and put it beside the David.

"Well, what's this then? You didn't say anything about another one, did you Charles?" Robert inquired.

I reeled off a little bit about the picture: the name of the sitter and the artist, and I could see Robert's wife was really taken with it.

"That's real smart of you, Charles, to have found that. I'm sure my Teresa would real like that, wouldn't you dear?" he said, turning to his wife.

I could see by her eyes she certainly would. "I'm glad, Robert," I replied, "because you're not buying that one."

"Oh, and why not?" Robert said with surprise.

"I'll tell you why, Robert. You and I have been good friends and done good business together. That's a little present from me to you and Teresa."

"Oh no, come on, Charles. We don't do this. We do business."

Shaking my head, I said: "I'm sorry, Robert, either it's that way or I take it away."

After about five minutes on these lines he accepted the present with:

"Well, I just don't know what to say ... But thanks Charles from Teresa and me." And his wife joined in: "Oh thanks, Charles, it's just so good of you."

I lifted out my package of drawings and prints and put them on a table. We hustled the packing-case back into his lumber-room. Then they couldn't wait any longer to show me round their home. First of all it was the dining-room and the living-room where the sporting pictures were hanging, and I must say they were framed and hung with taste. After this it was her room, and I thought the Spanish royal family and theirs looked quite at home. She even took me up to the little room where the still life and the flower painting were.

When Teresa (she had not been christened this, but apparently Robert had always called her it because it was a name she had liked much more than her own) brought me downstairs again Robert was sitting looking fixedly at the David. He turned:

"Charles, this just beats anything else you've ever done for me." He looked at his wife, "Now, my dear, could you perhaps get us a drink? Charles and I have just got to settle over this," pointing to the David.

When she had gone Robert continued:

"Well, I don't care really what it costs. This is the most wonderful thing that's happened to me, that I should own it and it's belonged to all those people in Europe right back in history. Now, Charles, come on, what's the figure?"

I told him the sum I had in mind; in pounds it was just into six figures, and in dollars it was a lot further. He didn't even draw a quick breath. He only went on:

"I don't mind telling you if you'd said double that I'd have paid you like a lamb. I guess my brief-case don't quite hold that lot. But tomorrow I'll get it for you."

The next day he did pay me. I never fathomed what his banking arrangements were or how he managed to get hold of this kind of money in cash.

I had the most enjoyable week with them both and at the end of it Robert managed to arrange the loan of a big Dodge for me. I took off on a trip that was going to last about three weeks. We arranged to meet on such and such a date in New York where they were going to put me up in their apartment and show me the town before I caught the boat back.

I set off to the west passing through part of the Shenandoah National Park and then Lexington and after this over the Appalachians. Looking back, I think it was West Virginia, the 'Mountain State', that gave me the most beautiful scenery I saw on my tour. The trees in the Appalachians were clothed in their fresh new foliage; cool slopes mantled with basswood and rhododendron. As the car climbed up the road, it seemed as though I were perhaps leaving today's America behind and going back into the old frontier life of the early nineteenth century. One almost expected, rounding a corner, to come across some forgotten pioneer, with his old long rifle over his shoulder, out hunting for his family.

Before I had gone over to America I had made out a list of dealers whom I thought might be interested in what I had to offer. They fell principally in two places, Chicago and New York, with one or two scattered around in Boston, Cleveland, and places like Toledo.

It was a pleasant drive. I stopped off for the nights when I felt like it. I got up when I felt like it. I really lazed along.

After coming down from the Appalachians I headed towards Charlestown and then on to Cincinnati, which lies mostly stuck on the end of the southern tip of Ohio. Nicknamed the 'Queen city of the West' by Longfellow, the town is the home of the Taft family. I just managed to find time to call in to see the admirable Taft Museum in Pike Street before crossing the state border and heading for Indianapolis for the next night.

I found like many another traveller that the 'hoosiers' have a hospitality which is as warm as any to be found around these parts. I had heard of this strange name 'hoosier' and in a bar I had to break in and ask them what it meant. Apparently, way back in pioneer days when a traveller on a horse rode by a log cabin in the backwoods, the owner of the cabin would peer through the door and call out a cheerful 'Whose there?' The dialect of Indiana to the traveller from afar was said to have sounded like 'hoosier', and so the name stuck.

Here again I stopped for a little tourism, as I felt I must take a look at the Indianapolis Five Hundred, the great speedway, and also pass an hour in the museum there.

The next day I drove the two hundred odd miles to Chicago and arrived after a short stop-off lunch at a quick-service counter.

America's second city has a population of some three and a half million plus. It holds up the bottom end of Lake Michigan. Chicago claims that it invented the sky-scraper, and they have certainly produced the finest examples of that type of architecture that I have seen, with the twin towers of Marina City on the bank of the Chicago river opposite the Loop. It was an experience I wouldn't have missed, for second-hand accounts of places never flesh them out into real things. In my mind's eye I suppose I had a compounded image of Chicago, a mixture of blood-stained stock-yards, sub-machine guns and the rest. But now the Union stock-yards had been cleaned up, there was nothing like the volume of livestock processed in the area, and I didn't hear any bursts of gunfire.

Chicago has many points of importance. It is the largest inland port in the world, with ships coming down from the St Lawrence Seaway, across the great Lakes. From my point of view, it certainly had one of the finest art collections I have seen and one of the best hung with the Art Institute. Going round a collection of this quality and size, one realizes that whatever Duveen and the rest did in their times, they unquestionably awoke and spread the desire and appreciation of fine things.

During the five days I was there I not only found practically all the dealers that I had noted down, but also found them friendly and ready to buy. In fact, by the end of my stay I had divested myself of very nearly two thirds of what I had brought over and sold them very handsomely indeed. The last afternoon I went shopping for I wasn't quite sure what, on the Miracle Mile, north of the Loop. After having a couple of hours' satisfying window gazing, I came away with nothing more exciting than a long focus lens for my camera.

The next stop off was Toledo. Driving through the 'Buckeye' state, I got off the main highways and shun-piked along the back roads which took me away from the principal industrial areas. The state gets its nickname from the tree which flourished in Ohio's forests. According to a Dr Daniel Drake, it must have been the be-and-end-all for the early settlers, as he has written that nearly everything could be made from this tree, from hats to venison trenchers, spoons, and bowls.

Toledo itself is really a town of glass, and the story of glass manufacture and history is well shown in the museum on Monro Street. Here also I had hoped to meet the odd dealer, but drew a blank.

From Toledo on along the southern shore of Lake Erie towards Cleveland. The most important events for me there were to divest myself of twelve more drawings, six etchings, two engravings, and to visit the outstanding Museum of Art. From here I pushed on to Buffalo and I just had to pander to the tourist in me, and out to Niagara.

I can only admit that the view from the top of the 282 foot Prospect Park Tower was a must, which I wouldn't have missed. From there one can see at the same time the thousand-foot-wide Canadian Horseshoe Falls. I went through it all. I took the elevator to the Cave of the Winds; staggered damply across the cat-walk at the base of the falls.

The trouble is, that America really is big. You can drive in the middle there for pretty well a thousand miles in any direction you like and you're not going to fall off it. It has so much that one lifetime completely devoted to it would never soak up all the extremes which you can meet.

I went on now heading east, through Rochester and Syracuse; and a couple of days later came into Boston, Massachusetts. With the whole place founded upon the rock at Plymouth where the Pilgrims landed December 16th 1620, there is probably as much history here as anywhere else in the States. Memories of Paul Revere, the old whalers chasing their private 'Moby Dicks', the Minutemen, the Tea Party. My main memory of Boston, however, is on a more mundane plain; that is, quite simply, the finest lobster I have ever had anywhere before or since. This was at one of those harbour-side restaurants. I did also take in the Museum of Fine Arts and that intriguing collection in the Isabella Stewart Gardner Museum. I was pleased too to find homes for forty-two drawings and prints, which left me about a hundred for New York – mental note, maybe sometime in the future I must try this jape again.

After three days in Boston I set off early for the last leg down to the capital and to meet up again with Robert.

There were just eight days left of my trip and I don't think ever in my life have I had so much crammed into such a period. Robert and his wife were indefatigable guides and for the first three of those days we did New York's art. Practically the whole of the first day went at the Met., which must bid fair to being the largest establishment of its kind in the world. It had yet to come to the painful moment in its history which was classed by some as 'de-accession and de-authentication time'. From there we went to the Guggenheim Museum, that rather extraordinary bulky corkscrew by Frank Lloyd Wright. On the next day it was the Frick with the outstanding examples of fourteenth- to nineteenth-century paintings, sculpture, furniture and textiles. After that came the private galleries.

When visiting these Robert most tactfully stayed apparently deeply engrossed with some exhibit in the front room whilst I went and made my number with my brief-case. By the time we had visited the fifth of these private establishments I was cleaned. Nothing left. But I had in place a very nice bundle of the green and crackly.

During the remaining time Robert and his wife took me in their car on a number of out-of-town expeditions. We went down to Montauk, which is on the far tip of Long Island. Robert explained to me that this was where fishermen came to take to the water for some of the best swordfish and tuna fishing. We passed through Amagansett, which is part of the Hamptons – big white houses snug behind the green hedges, the hideouts of those who make the Hamptons tick.

I was very pleased when he took me to a number of bookshops he knew and left me to browse, and amongst these I turned out some titles that would add quite markedly to my library at home. The parcels made a fairly heavy lump, but they would pass for hand baggage for the trip back. During that week I was also taken either by them both or by Robert alone to sample several restaurants, and I must say for diversity and quality they put New York high up in any league – places like the Four Seasons, which Robert told me had only been open a few years. Well, they packed in as much as they could for me, and when the morning of my embarkation arrived I really can't say that it was with joy that I strapped up my bags. They took me down to the Cunard pier. My luggage was handed over to the porter with the cabin details and the rest. We said our farewells, and with a flurry of waves over my shoulder I followed in the trail of the porter.

*   *   *

On the trip back there was only one happening of importance. I met up with an interesting Japanese. He like many of his countrymen was beginning to gather together what might be called 'Westerniana'. In the years since then it has been fascinating for me to read sale reports and to see just how much money his people are spending and what they are buying with it: paintings, furniture; in fact, almost all of the top artifacts of Western civilization. But then, after all we in the West go dollar and pound crazy over Ming vases and Hiroshige prints.

Anyway the gentleman I met was ambitious and had a cheque book to match. During the crossing we had some lengthy and involved discussions, which as far as I was concerned brought good profit in the years that were to follow. My friend from the Land of the Rising Sun had an unusual taste and set me a number of problems to satisfy it. I can recall some truly alarming telephone conversations with him when he got back to Japan. At times these became highly involved when he was trying to get across his meaning to me as to what he wanted and his grip of English failed him, and when I would be subjected to a torrent of words in Japanese, French, English and German. I have never been to Japan and in many ways I wish I had. I would like to visit my friend's establishment to see how his new acquisitions look hanging in the reflected light from Fujiyama.

*   *   *

In December of 1964 I gave Robert my customary call. I was greeted not by him but by his wife with some very sad news. She told me that in the fall he and a party of friends had gone off on a shooting expedition to Canada. There had been a bad accident and Robert had been shot. She said:

"I don't know, Charles. . . . This is some weeks back now. I guess I am trying hard to begin to get over the shock. I'm selling up over here and moving myself and a few bits and pieces away, perhaps over to Spain. I'm still trying to sort myself out and decide what to do."

Well, there went a nice person and certainly one of the best of my clients.

* * *

1965, and I was carrying on business as usual, but I was also toying with the idea of perhaps operating on a rather higher level. Museums and galleries. I suppose to someone in my profession they stand out like Kilimanjaro, Everest or one of those frozen sharp inaccessible peaks in the Andes. They are there to be taken. I could afford to take my ease now and really study this problem of galleries and museums.

I approached it rather in the manner I had often done in the war when coming up against something I wasn't quite sure about. I learnt then that if survival were the object, I must try and recognize all the plus points and look most carefully for the minus marks.

I realized I didn't *have* to pull any more jobs. But then – the taste kept coming back. So, I started to build up a dossier, which I continue to add to all the time, concerning these public show-cases all over the world. I already knew the principal contents of many and I am always endeavouring to keep up to date by means of every avenue at my disposal.

The contents of museums and galleries, from my point of view, present an interesting exercise. It is clear that whether these places take advantage of it or not, a very considerable arsenal of sophisticated alarms and warning devices is available these days. There is always the rider, of course, if they can afford it. Yet it still seems surprising how comparatively few of the whole international scene have anything substantial in the way of a protective system.

Bearing in mind all the possibilities I could think of, I started working on various exercises, mental exercises. For instance, guards on duty in rooms where I might wish to remove a picture. Here I worked round an idea based on diversion. I think it first came to me when I was wandering round Darmstadt Zoo one afternoon. I was captivated by the antics of one of the very small monkey family. The thought crossed my mind as to whether it might be possible to work out a distracting episode using one of these as my 'assistant'. Sometime after the visit to Darmstadt I questioned an acquaintance who was associated with circuses and animals in particular. How easy would it be, I asked him, to train this particular type of monkey. His reply was that in individual cases with this breed training was a comparatively simple matter. Such a one could quite reliably be set to go through a simple routine it had learnt thoroughly.

Following up this idea, I thought about procuring one of these little monkeys and training it at home to create a diversion, such as jumping and climbing on to a picture-frame and then starting to jabber. With a few more refinements this manoeuvre might serve to draw away attention from an object I had in mind lifting by bringing nearby guards and people to find out what the rumpus was about. Meanwhile I could make off with what I wanted. I would probably have to sacrifice my little friend or rather leave him to be taken to a zoo or cared for otherwise.

As I delved deeper into the question of diversion tactics bearing in mind the possiblity of running into pictures which were alarmed with an anti-touch device, I found some interesting facts. On investigation, it became clear that only in special cases would individual paintings be alarmed back to the switchboard. The more general practice was to have them in relays of up to about ten on the same circuit. These ten might not necessarily be all in the same room or on the same floor. For this set-up I didn't think in terms of employing a monkey. The device I had in mind was a simple spring mechanism which could be held in a contracted position by some form of wire and acid contraption, rather on the lines of a delayed motion fuse such as I'd come across during the war.

The principle would be that I could go to a gallery where they had a room which at times was unattended. Here, very, very gently this device could be slipped between the frame and the wall, which should be possible as the touch alarm systems generally only respond to a vibration from the canvas or the panel itself. Before slipping it in I would trigger off the acid action which would start eating through the retaining wire and then go along to the room where the picture was that I wanted which would be on the same relay as the one being disturbed. When the wire was eaten through the device would go off with sufficient force to give the frame a good shake; this would set off the 'touch' alarm which would at the same time break the relay for that group of ten pictures, meaning that the others in this set could be lifted off without giving any additional warning.

As good as any of these security gadgets may be, as regards galleries and museums a good deal of the responsi-bility must surely fall on the personnel, certainly during daylight hours; and anybody who has been in charge of some operation knows only too well that it is a fundamental difficulty to keep people on top-line incessantly. They are almost bound to come down and lose watchfulness and observation.

Considering the possibilities of roughing up galleries and museums, very early in my career I had almost instinctively set out to visit every feasible institution in these categories wherever I went, and when doing so had made it a habit surreptitiously to make sketches and take notes of the placing of rooms and general lay-out, etcetera. At the same time I always helped myself to any available published material that would aid me in making reasonably accurate plans of the place afterwards. Needless to say, I keep these all carefully filed away.

I carried out one experiment about a year or two ago when I was visiting such an establishment. This one had large main gallery rooms, and off them quite small side-chambers which had on show the smaller pictures. There was a charming little Dutch interior on copper. The picture only measured about five inches by seven and it was in a narrow frame not much more than an inch wide; it was secured to the wall just by means of a form of clip that opened by pressure. I was wearing an overcoat which had been made for me specially at one time with two cavernous poachers' pockets that could only be reached from inside. I slipped the little Dutch picture into one of these pockets and walked out with no trouble.

Towards the end of the sixties, art thefts certainly began to boom. Over the years I have amassed an appreciable dossier on thefts, because it is always interesting to see what the competition is up to. Certainly since 1969 I've done it almost as an academic exercise. What exactly is the recovery rate is not a published fact, although we in the trade have a fair idea. It's not very high. I've known for some time too that there are those operators who take with the sole idea in mind of blackmailing the insurance companies for a ransom. They've had their successes. The taking business is also most probably helped particularly by the owners themselves; for, as has been pointed to earlier, very few go in for any kind of security. On occasion, as I know myself, it can be easy to keep track of what they own – it can cost as little as just a pint for the gardener in the local.

Certainly there are some daring characters operating in this field and as the security devices increase, so do the techniques for breaking them. I can amuse myself by flicking through some of their activities, such as the breaking of a story on June 22nd 1969 about a theft of paintings from the Queen's collection. Six pictures had been taken from the Lord Chamberlain's Office in St James's Place, where they had been stored. For almost a year after, the theft remained undiscovered. It was only when four of the pictures were handed into Christie's, which is after all only a few yards from St James's Palace, to be sold that it was discovered where they had come from. It is thought the pictures may have changed hands many times after the theft. A little later the police recovered the other two. A spokesman from Buckingham Palace said 'The whole thing is a mystery, the pictures are all quite small and might easily have been smuggled out underneath somebody's coat, or in large pockets.' I'm not the only one to use this method!

An example of medium-sized really high quality pictures just disappearing came in June 1970. These were taken from an address in London. 'Nature Mort au Pommes et aux Raisin' by Paul Gauguin and 'Deux Chaises dans le Jardin' by Pierre Bonnard. They are worth around the quarter of a million pounds mark. Five years missing with no sign. Even with a reward of £17,500 or pro rata to be paid for information leading to the recovery of these paintings being offered by Douglas Jackson and Company (Adjusters) Ltd., of London and New York.

But for sheer volume I don't think there is a country that can compete with Italy. On one of my trips there I gleaned some useful information. This was during the attending of various functions and meeting people high up in the art world. I was told, for instance, that there are still well over a thousand works of art that went missing in the war that haven't yet turned up. I couldn't help wondering if any of those that I had 'come across' were on this list. I made especial note of the operations of Rodolfo Siviero who was heading the Delegation for the recovery of Italian Works of art Abroad. I saw in the press that he had admitted that thousands, perhaps tens of thousand of works of art were leaving Italy illegally every year, and among these were many objects that were priceless. Signore Siviero was also involved with the matter of the 'Portrait of a Young Girl' by Raphael which reached the Museum of Fine Arts in Boston via a somewhat odd purchase from a dealer near Genoa. (I couldn't help wondering if this was my contact in that area – I just couldn't be sure.) The Raphael is now back in Italy.

Indubitably the goings on in Italy seem particularly numerous and diverse. There are side-lines too to this issue like the one in 1973 when some men entered a Rome church and tied up the priest and the sexton, bundling them into a confessional box and as they struggled helplessly, made off with three paintings worth more than a million pounds.

In my somewhat bulky reference section I have yet another folio and this is on security devices which I have tried to keep right up to date as the years have gone by. I must admit that today the variation and cunning of them does sometimes make me think twice about any place which I know or suspect has such protection. However, you can't always be sure if you see a firm's alarm strapped rather obviously to the front of a building that it is actually protected, because it is not unknown for some people to think it sufficient if they just have the unconnected alarm bell outside, as a put-you-off.

To collect details of security devices is not quite as difficult as it sounds, as the firms marketing and fitting these devices are rather caught between two fires. Obviously they want to have satisfied customers, but to get these customers they have to advertise. I have found on occasion that I have been able myself to get information from them fairly simply.

A good deal of security protection harks back to some of the work I was doing in the war, with booby-traps and other assorted hardware that had to be cleared. The end result then if a mistake were made was rather more permanent than it is today; but the principle is roughly the same. The security people like the enemy do their best to hide whatever gadgets they are using. But the finest systems it seems can occasionally be totally defeated at the outset if it is possible to pick up 'leaks' as to what they are and where they are fitted.

As to getting into a building if defences have been fitted, I am constantly reminding myself of some of the difficulties I may expect. Doors can have what is called closed circuit, double-pole, electrical wiring at four-inch centres, and this can also be extended to wall areas. The system provides a continuous current of electricity across the protected area which is so designed to actuate the alarm immediately it is broken. There can also be all kinds of electronic devices fitted to the door-locks themselves. Windows can have vibration contacts that are fitted on to the glass and activated as soon as the glass itself is broken. I have come across what are called knock out tubes; these are provided to protect the glass. They are placed into position at night and are designed to complete an electrical circuit by holding a contact in position; if they are disturbed the circuit is broken and off goes the alarm; in the day-time these tubes are taken away.

Once inside a building a whole battery of instrumentation can be met with. This can range from simple pressure pads which are strategically placed in so-called 'trap' positions beneath carpet or lino, which go off when sufficient weight is applied to them. But I have managed to deal with some of these.

The items that I really felt I should especially know about are the rays that use modulated invisible light beams. These can be effective to a distance of up to two hundred feet. The trouble with them is that sometimes they take quite a bit of spotting. They can be easily camouflaged. Depending on the angle of acceptance, at times it can be possible to crawl underneath them; it is rather a risky procedure, but I have done it.

A nastier one still to defeat is the microwave intrusion detector. This is generally adjustable for a cigar-shaped field of surveillance, stretching in between ten and thirty feet from the generator. It has a refinement; the selectivity of the detector is enhanced by filters in the equipment amplifier; these gadgets select the correct Doppler frequency so that the instrument will only respond to movements that have a human characteristic.

There are a whole range of master keys and shunt switches, which are generally activated by a little box near the outside door. The lid of this is opened by a special key and then there are two small knobs inside. When the owner goes out he scrambles the combination of two figures by turning these knobs. This activates the whole system of protection, which can include devices such as those that have been mentioned earlier. When he comes back he opens the box with his key and then turns the two knobs to the correct combination, which will neutralize the whole protection system, allowing him to enter. This has to be done correctly the first time; if not, off goes the whole bag of tricks; incidentally as with most of these alarms, it rings in the police station or security firm's office and not in the house. The fault with these shunt switch devices, as far as I can see, is that the combination is too simple with only two figures – that is, of course, if it's my property that is being protected; the other way round, it's fine.

I came across one of these in the Munich area not long ago. The incident was a slightly complicated affair. I was prospecting for my Japanese contact for some rather off-beat early twentieth-century work he wanted – he also had Soutine high on the list. I was in Munich because on going through my index-books I had found out where the pictures he needed were hanging. I also knew what the owner looked like, as I had come across a cutting with a photograph of him attending the opera – underneath it had said that he was an indefatigable opera goer and always attended first nights; it also added some other details about him, including he was a leading industrialist, which I already knew, and was an avid collector of the arts, which I also knew.

So I was going to attend a first night at the opera in Munich. Further thought suggested I should have someone with me for introductions. I had had some business with an owner of a private gallery and in the way one does had become superficially friendly with him. If he were available and willing, he would do. It worked. He'd love to come to the opera. (I found out definitely, although I had decided it must be so, that he did know the man I wanted to be introduced to. I did this surreptitiously of course.) We arranged to be at the opera in four days' time for the forthcoming first night. We arrived in the turmoil of the foyer and I sighted my quarry. Further, I found that our seats were only four rows behind where he was sitting, apparently alone.

They do the interval business at the Munich Opera House very well. There was an excellent buffet and an array of bottles with a reasonable amount of space to move around. The time between the acts proved adequate for me to encourage my gallery friend to introduce me, which he did and gratuitously gave a mini ad lib biography regarding my tastes and activities as a connoisseur – as he thought he understood them. The three of us arranged to meet in the next interval. We did, and over more drinks the industrialist asked us back after the opera as he would like to show me his collection. Fortunately, the gallery owner excused himself; but I said I should be delighted.

After the final curtain I joined up with the industrialist, who said that first we must have some supper. For him this proved to be, apart from a little savoury fish, mostly liquid. Somewhere near one o'clock he called for the bill and we left. As he was going past my hotel, I suggested that I pick up my car and then follow him out.

When we arrived at his place, which lay to the south of the city, he parked his car and signalled me to draw into the large garage beside him. On our approaching the front door, I saw that he had one of these shunt switch gadgets. He just managed to get the key into the lock with much wavering of a hand shaking from so many large Scotches. When it opened there was a terrific lot of confused counting in German. Eventually I gathered from all this that his combination was 54, which he proceeded to dial, and just about made it. Once in the hall he threw down his keys on to a salver on an oak chest. Almost at once he suggested showing me round his collection of which he was obviously extremely proud, and had some reason to be.

I noted that the three items the Jap wanted were there. I also made particular note of something else that was important. The German, who was now too far gone in his cups for his own good, showed me at this point an important early Italian painting which I knew quite well had been stolen about two years before. Just to complete matters for me so far, he told me he had to go away the next day for a week. He then proceeded to get rather maudlin, and told me how he lived alone with all his treasures.

As the night wore on he became more and more far gone. I, needless to say, was staying good and sober. In the vapour of the Scotch he was fortunately seeing me more and more in the light of some long lost friend. Eventually, at some time past two, he suggested I should stay the night, imagining that I was the drunk one. This suited me extremely well, as an idea had already started shaping in my mind in which a pair of splendid brown beeswax candles on the mantelpiece played a part, and which his suggestion would make more feasible. After apparently a little persuasion I acquiesced to his idea and we climbed the stairs arm in arm. He insisted he lent me some of his silk pyjamas, which I myself thought would be a bit voluminous and short for my figure, but accepted with the necessary appreciation; after which he showed me into a rather sumptuous room across the landing from the one he was to retire into – I could have wished his and my rooms had been farther apart, but no matter.

There was much bumping around from behind his door and then silence for a few minutes until a stentorian snoring struck up with a slow and steady rhythm.

I waited until three fifteen, whereupon I sock-footed my way downstairs by the light of a small pen-torch. I picked up his keys from the salver and made for the beeswax candles. With the help of the latter I took some excellent impressions of the shunt-key and the door-key. To make things look more normal I cut off equal pieces from the bottoms of both candles and replaced them. He'd never notice the difference the next morning. I cleaned the keys and put the bunch back on the salver, and returned to my room.

The next morning my host surfaced enough to provide us with orange juice and coffee. After this he packed his bag and in our separate cars we drove off.

During the day I arranged to have keys made by a warped locksmith whom I had used on an earlier occasion. The night after that I paid a visit and did my stuff with the dialling system. I did, however, take the elementary precaution after dialling of retreating into some nearby undergrowth and waiting a whole hour just in case the cunning chap might have had some complication with the alarm gear and my efforts would call up the polizei. They didn't come. He hadn't.

Other security gadgets I have also come close to encountering are the so-called inertia switches, and devices for detecting vibration caused by entry be it ever so slight. I was rather intrigued by one of the advertisements for these things; it had an illustration showing a thermic lance cutting through eighteen inches of concrete on which an inertia switch had been placed. The switch did pick up the vibrations of the lance. But so far I haven't tried carting round one of these lance gadgets and I haven't heard of anyone who has.

Bearing in mind what I said earlier about the publicity attached to liftings from galleries and museums and the fact that it is likely an increasing number of these places will as time goes on be going in for this kind of refined protection if they can get the money to do so, only serves to underline my decision made some years back that it is necessary to step very lightly where such establishments are concerned especially the big ones or the very special ones. Actually I find plenty of gravy working the other places.

There is also another point concerning museums and galleries, and this is that in most countries they now have fairly comprehensive documentation as to their collections, such as, serial cards on which can be a description of the object, any particular inscriptions, details of any damages, maybe a sketch and a photograph. Thank goodness, as a rule not many private owners take advantage of such precautions which if they only knew would help them against the likes of me to trace and get back their treasures in some instances. But I hope when too many cotton on to this idea by then I shall have definitely retired.

Yet all the expertise and instrumentation in the world can be brought to its knees by the human element. I had a perfect example of this in March 1970. One of the snags of my profession is the procuring of accurate information. I know I have all my files, dossiers, and the rest, but inevitably these have gaps in them, which I am always looking out for an opportunity to fill. The hitting in the dark method is not for me. Let the quick-quid lads go for ringing bells, looking through windows and so on. That way I am quite sure is bound to fail in the long run.

The incident I am referring to happened, or rather started to happen, when I was having a snack and drink at lunchtime in the Lord Raglan in St Martins-le-Grand round the back of St Paul's. It was one of those rather pleasant early spring days and the city was waking up from the frosts and the muck of the winter. I was sitting behind a well-chilled pint of lager and idly scanning the *Financial Times* when a mini-skirted raven-locks and her fellow, tight-jeaned, wispy, be-jewelled with a fake Iron Cross and three foot of brass chain sat down on the opposite side of the table. She was very soon nosing into a Babycham, trying not to swallow the cherry; he sucked inexpertly at a horrible half of lager and blackcurrant cordial.

What brought me up with a jerk was her third attempt at conversation with Iron Cross.

"Corr . . . broke two bloody nails this morning; that greasy little sod of a manager had me typing two hours solid on some frigging survey of a mansion and its bloody contents."

Iron Cross, who was bored, responded: "Well, why don't you do something in the groove? . . . Where's a sodding insurance office going to get you. 'Bout all you're fit for."

Raven-locks flared: "All right Mr Know-it-clever with all your quid from the building site. Takes half an hour on the dance floor till the dust stops falling out."

"Oh roll it up, bird." Iron Cross poured the rest of his lager and blackcurrant equally down his throat and shirt front and stamped out. Raven-locks called after him. "You want to watch you don't go rusty." Then she turned back to finish her Babycham; went across to the bar to return with a second. Sat down and went into the inevitable nail, eyebrow, lips routine.

I'd been slow; this was a way I had never cottoned on to before. Thirty years or more ago I could recall my father would have just rung his broker and asked for a cover and that would have been that with just a few details; none of this survey business and detailed contents list. Jobs for the boys that could make security as leak-proof as a colander.

Slick little lads with twopence worth of spiel and knowledge screwed from a paperback on Chippendale and Titian.

This called for a try. I looked her over. Possible. She was fresh and fleshy, her thirty-six cups were at that moment still in the process of shaking as her pique died down. The easiest way would be to do the old 'knock over the glass' trick . . . lots of sorry and have another one. But I was beaten to it. As I turned over a page, a rather stilted little voice broke through the insidious garbage of taped music, or rather noise, which the brewers seem to imagine we like and will help to sell more wallop for them.

"Excuse me . . . have you a light?" I glanced up to meet raven-locks' eyes passing me all of two kilowatts in a carefully rehearsed and copied manner of some flickering fairy from the box. I reached into my side pocket and flicked my lighter towards the slightly shaking tip of her cigarette.

"Thanks." She inhaled heavily and too deeply and went into a paroxysm. As the spluttering ceased, she collected herself quickly and winked across the table. "Ruddy fags these days." Then with scarcely a pause sailed into the assault. "Come here often? Don't think I've seen you before."

"If I'm in the city," I replied.

She must have been doing some speedy homework on her own account, for her eyes were saying things about two fences ahead of her lips. "You work around here?"

"Not really, I just come up here now and then."

"I know where you've been. That's as lovely a tan that didn't come out of no tube. . . . I went package to one of them Spanish places last year. Sun's all right. Can't say I go much on their idea of food though. Besides you want the right company. Turned out a proper drudge with him," looking towards the door where Iron Cross had made his exit.

Her glass was empty again and I took it across with my own for a refill. When I returned she was warming to her idea, which I hoped could be linked to my idea.

"I bet you aren't stuck in an office all day?"

"No, thank goodness."

"Cheers then."

Her quite attractive little nose jostled the cherry in the glass.

"I expect you're a farmer or something?"

"No, I'm not so good early in the morning with cows and milk; the sight of all those udders would do terrible things to my breakfast."

She giggled at the thought. " 'Spect you travel then for some firm?"

"Travel . . . yes . . . But not really for a firm."

I could sense that little computer behind the dark green eyes was spinning away to get some assessment of how many pounds this might mean. A little fabrication on my part was called for to set matters towards what I was after.

A speedy run through possibilities and then it flashed up.

"Actually, I'm in films."

To me, when I said it, it sounded like pure corn. But the effect on raven-locks was close to devastating. The thirty-six cups started up again and she nearly swallowed her cigarette. "Well, I . . ." It had thrown her stroke. "Do . . . do you mean you're on them?" She almost whispered with venerating intensity.

"Oh no, I'm the other side of the cameras, on the directing angle. Most of my time is taken up on finding locations."

Part of her interest seemed to wane and then it returned.

"You – you met many of them – the stars I mean?"

"Quite a few in the last ten years."

She glanced down at her watch. "Oh hell. I gotta rush. You couldn't come along here again when I'm out of the office?"

It was all go with her. I wasn't quite sure whether Edward ought to touch the brakes – No!

"I've a better idea. I'm on my own for company. How are you fixed for dinner?"

Before she answered I could see the lad was going to have a lovely time with his Iron Cross chain and all, standing waiting outside for the never never.

"Well, yes, I could."

"How about seven thirty? There's a little place a friend introduced me to. You know Tottenham Court Road. A bit up on the left, Percy Street." I then told her the name of the restaurant. She was all and ready for the net.

"Oh I'll be there . . . and its Rina."

"I'm Peter," I replied, producing another from the list of possible aliases.

"See you then . . . Peter." And she was gone back to that office with the greasy little manager.

Just occasionally one is under the trees when the fruit falls. I had a few hours to make up some background for the cover story, and to concoct a little seasoning and add a carrot or two. I was going to rake through my memories of the lurid Sundays that were nearly always larded with the old ham of 'through the bed to your name in lights'. In some moods Mr Mitty was very close to my heart. There is something in playing a part that makes the red fellows race through the veins. Thanks be that my way along the road was never dull. I could always take to a side play with zest. Deception, the curtain to these affairs that came and went, was part of me by now.

I downed the last of the lager and went out to call a cab to return to the staid façade of my West End hotel. This operation was going to have certain degrees of ruthlessness about it.

The flash effect of my announcement that came up in Rina's eyes reflected the rather sad state of hope so many of the tens of thousands of Rinas live in. They are suspended in a cocoon of synthetic desire fabricated from the lowest denomination programmes beamed out of those rectangular mesmerizing screens. Ideas for dreams from the mass of circulated magazines, always the glamour was dangled just out of reach. Each shot in the evening would get them through the days of office boredom.

What Rina didn't know was that what she idled her way through in a glaze of irksome monotony was steak, veg and gravy to me. One of the troubles I have is patience. Get on to an idea and it must be now. But need during the years had led me to build up some sort of blocking system, so that I found I could slow matters down.

I met Rina for dinner. It was the beginning of a period spent mostly with her having dinner with me, or back in her little one-roomed flatlet in Streatham with me having nights with her. During all this time I spun a web of promise across the stars for the poor little thing. I didn't think much of myself for doing it. But the information she passed back to me, which she thought was supplying my need for film locations, backed up with what she was certain would be the promise of some small bit part for her to start with, made it all worth while to her.

If some of those speculating sons in the insurance business had heard a fraction of the accurate information Rina gave me, not only verbally but also accompanied with those handy photo-copies, they would have been out of the insurance lark and quick. A lifted Rembrandt may not sound off the 'Lutine' but some gambling lad is going to have to shell out.

Passion seemed to work a release mechanism in Rina, because during these Streatham nights she also let out quite gratuitously so much of the whole pattern of security for her firm which I thought must be one of the biggest groups. Certainly, from the list of mansions, castles, etcetera that she quoted me, to say the least, she was putting a very generous slice of property in jeopardy.

*   *   *

The house and garden now looked very different from when I had bought them. Inside my furnishing was complete if such a thing can ever be. The wood sheened warmly from the beeswax and the hand of my friend who looked after that with the same care and devotion as she did me and my needs. The walls bore the results of some purchases that I had made, mostly culled from sales at Christie's and Sotheby's, where my agent had bid for me. It may sound rather strange that I should buy pictures; but it would be scarcely wise for me to stick up those that I had acquired by other means. Anyway I have never been one for large works, preferring mostly sketches and drawings, which are sometimes more readily readable to myself, and with these I can perhaps analyse them and join in with the artist as I sense him working out some small idea.

Outside, the garden, after a number of years of care and planting, now gave me a great sense of satisfaction. The one who was responsible for this and who gave of his knowledge and time to turn it into a minor showpiece picked up my appreciation. There was hardly a month of the year when some bloom on plant or shrub wasn't in evidence. The orchard was bearing well.

Towards the end of the year I felt the yen to visit my

contact near Genoa again as I hadn't been near him for
some time. So down to the south and along the coast road
into Italy. The air down there was a heady mixture of
various harvest left-overs and there was still a pleasant
warmth in the late afternoons. Driving through the hills on
the other side of Genoa, I arrived at his place just as dusk
was rolling in down the valleys. He was in fine fettle
although the years of good feeding must by now be costing
him a good many lire in tailor's bills. After just one glass of
wine he was handing me a shopping-list the contents of
which were urgently needed. As far as I could gather, most
of his other suppliers had lost interest or were taking wise
holidays on the other side of the globe. He mentioned one
or two private collectors who had the kind of things he
wanted. Then, as an afterthought, he asked me to be on the
look out for a good Holy Family, which I thought was an
odd way to put it.

I spent nearly three weeks cruising round Italy; even
crossed over to Sicily for a couple of days. By the time I
came back to my friend I had a useful bag for him;
including works by Albani, Guardi, Longhi, Piazzetta,
Sebastiano Ricci and Sodoma.

*　　*　　*

It was May 1972 and I had just returned from a foray
across to England and into Scotland making profitable use
of some of the information Rina had passed me. This was
the third time that I had been able to follow up her helpful
hints. I was interested to note that there didn't seem, so far,
to be an instance when there was evidence of tightening up
in security or alterations to any of the systems that she had
described. I can only imagine that poor Rina had not spilled
the beans or been caught out.

This latest batch included a number of delightful miniatures. Here again I was up against temptation. Some of the results that have come my way have almost begged me to keep them for my personal enjoyment. But too risky for long – I only allow myself a brief flirtation with them, and then like other things they must go. Yet when I looked at these miniatures and took a magnifying glass to them I revelled in the technical brilliance of the early English painters who had accomplished this work. The fantastic accuracy of their brush strokes, every hair, eye-lash in place; and the way that some of them had included in the jewellery minute fragments of precious stones and tiny pieces of gold leaf, so that the whole – often only about two or three inches across – had a gem-like quality.

After having had my moment of adoration I packed them up and the next day set off for the long drive to see my Alsace friend. I stopped for the night in the rather dreary town of Épinal; the main reason being that I was tired and couldn't be bothered to go any farther that day. After a scratch meal in the station buffet I decided to have a saunter round to clear my head from the fumes and dust of the roads. Épinal has not much to boast about; it does make Kirsch, which is a plus mark; it is also noted as a centre for the production of cheap engravings and lithographs. The growth of the place starts from the founding of a monastery by the Bishop of Metz in the tenth century. It got itself ceded to the duchy of Lorraine in 1465 and then became part of France in the eighteenth century.

Just after eleven-thirty that night I was returning to my hotel down a series of deserted side streets when some rather shady movements and noises stopped me and flicked a reflex actiom to step into a convenient deep doorway. I could just make out a couple of figures about forty yards down the street on the other side who were engaged in wrapping something up and putting whatever the something was in the back of a large American shooting-brake. What light there was came reflected from the centre of the town and it was not a great help. As the lads were showing no lights to aid them with their efforts my curiosity was aroused.

They were now filling up the rest of the back of the brake with what looked like cushions and pillows. When this was completed they locked up the vehicle and went round carefully trying all the doors and then started to come down the street towards me. The doorway I had chosen fortunately had a wicket door that was not secured and I managed without making a noise to slip in behind the door. As they came past where I was hidden I caught a scrap of talk which indicated they were just going to have a snack and then were coming back to drive off across to . . . the rest of what they said was lost as they turned a corner and headed probably for the station buffet which seemed to be the only place likely to be open.

I waited till their footsteps had died away and then catlike with curiosity I crept up to the brake. The locks, like most car locks, were about as pick-proof as a child's cheap money box. I got the tail-gate open and fumbled down through the mass of pillows and cushions until I came to the package they were so keen on concealing. It was possible to slide it out and my itching fingers soon gave the message that it contained pictures. Rearranging the pillows and cushions I relocked the tail-gate and went off in the opposite direction to which the two lads had gone. Reaching the hotel by a circuitous route, I locked the package in my estate car.

The next morning out in the country I stopped in a sheltered nook and peeped to see what the chaps had given me. Surprise, surprise, I found myself the owner of a fine Frans Hals and a lively portrait by Peter Paul Rubens. I had visions of the panic stations my donors would be going to when they arrived at their destination or maybe had gone to in the early hours of the morning if they had checked to see if their loot was still under the pillows and cushions. I spent the main part of that day taking the odd glass of wine in various cafés and bars but nevertheless ended up arriving in the vicinity of Herr Alsace at the time I intended.

When I got to him, which was around six in the evening, he was more than usually pleased to see me. The matter of purchasing what I had brought went through with the greatest ease, and I didn't even feel inclined to push up the price he offered. After such matters were finished, he took me by my arm and led me across to a room I had never been in before. It was surprisingly well furnished, in good taste. On the walls, a little unexpectedly perhaps, some good early maps interspersed with Wenceslaus Hollar prints. He pointed me to a chair and then went across to a drinks cabinet and this time, I noticed, poured me out an astonishingly generous wallop.

During the next hour and two more drinks, and two cigars supplied by him, he discoursed on art, architecture and taste. As he warmed to his subjects, he became less nervous; he almost lost that tiresome habit of the continual clearing of the throat. I found that to a slight degree I was warming towards him. At the end of the hour he said: "I hope you will have some dinner with me. When I saw you coming up the drive I sent my housekeeper out to get extra food, just in case. It will be a simple meal. It will give me pleasure."

I accepted and about a quarter of an hour later the room door opened and the housekeeper came in and announced that the meal was ready. He led me into the dining-room, a rather austere place, which was heavily draped in dark donkey grey velvet curtains. The wall-paper was lightly striped grey and silver to go with the curtains. The sole adornment on the walls was an elaborate near Chippendale gilt mirror over the fireplace and opposite to this was a small triptych – I guessed School of Cologne or some distant follower of Grünewald.

The meal was pickled herrings, followed up by a quite delicious venison steak, not too high, perfectly cooked with a matching fruit sauce, and with this a red vintage of quality. At the end cheese and fruit. He told the housekeeper, as she cleared away the other dishes, that that would be all and to leave the coffee with him. After she had gone he poured out the coffee and pushed the bottle of Asbach across to me. We lit cigars, and then he turned to me. "I expect you are wondering," and he gave a little slow smile. I didn't answer. he went on, "I have what could be an interesting proposition to talk over with you." I nodded looking him straight in the eyes and saw nothing that troubled me. He continued, "We have done business together now for . . . it is more than twenty years. . . . I think you know me a little. . . . I know nothing about you other than you always bring me good stuff and there have never, as far as I know, been any strings on the deals." He took a fair old mouthful of Asbach and pumped it down to his stomach, and came to the point. It was an interesting proposition. In brief, he had been manoeuvring for sometime an exchange of paintings with a contact in East Germany. He had eight pictures that they wanted and they had ten which he needed to get hold of, as he had an important client for them. As far as the contact in East Germany was concerned, it would be a straight exchange with what he was sending for what they would be bringing. As far as he was concerned and I was concerned, it would be a profitable exercise because the client for these ten pictures was prepared to pay a figure that was considerably more than Mr Alsace had had to pay for the paintings he was sending in exchange. There was the point, however, of the delivery to the contact. The deal had been finalized only about a month ago and he had been puzzled as to whom he was going to trust with the mission. He, of course, himself was now really past such things and more than this, he did not want the risk of being recognized as being involved in such matters. There were a number of people who brought him objects, but how many of these could he trust with what was a very valuable property? Either they could take off with the pictures he was sending or they could make off with the more valuable paintings coming from the other way and doublecross him. He wondered if I would think about it?

I asked first of all, "How big are these pictures that you are sending?" He said, "That is a good point. Come – we will see them." He led me to a small, locked box-room off the hall and, opening the door, showed them to me. They were all of the fifteenth- and sixteenth-century German School and the largest of them was not more than about twenty-six by twenty inches; they were all wood panels; and all packed together as one parcel it wouldn't be very bulky. He told me those coming the other way were not a great deal bigger. We went back into the lounge, and as I assimilated the second Asbach I tried to collect all the mental radar signals I had been and was receiving. After about five minutes I told him that I was prepared to do it. At this point, to save me the trouble of asking, he told me what my cut would be; quite honestly, it was a third of what he was going to make from the deal. He had after all had the trouble of getting everything together and making all the arrangements. The third was a good figure and the spice of the idea appealed to me.

The meeting place was to be Coburg and he would start final arrangements with the East German contact right away. He said if I could give him a call on a number which he wrote down on a piece of paper for me, in ten days' time he would have the instructions; he also said that I would have full descriptions of the pictures I was to pick up and photographs of them. There would be some form of password for recognition, and if possible he would try to have some description of the person I was to meet.

* * *

In ten days' time I had rung the number. He told me all was ready and the meeting would be in three days' time in the evening. I had already worked out distances. I told him that I would leave early in the morning of the day after tomorrow and should be with him about half past two to three o'clock in the afternoon.

By just after three I was drawing off the road and into the seclusion of the drive in front of Alsace's house. He had everything top-line. He handed me the quite copious descriptive notes, and also the photographs not only of the whole paintings but some details of specific parts. He wished me luck and we agreed to meet hopefully in a further two days' time.

I drove across country until I was able to pick up the E4 and followed this to just south of Heidelberg where I could branch off to the E12. This led me by easy motoring through Heilbronn, Crailsheim, Ansbach to Nuremberg. Here I turned away to the north aiming for Bamberg, where I intended to spend the night. The hotel had conveniently been able to find me a lock-up garage and I arranged to stay with them the next night as well.

The following morning, after a leisurely breakfast, I decided to put the evening's business out of my mind for a couple of hours and take a look around the town, which was new to me.

The cathedral is fine not only for the equestrian statue of the 'Knight of Bamberg', but also for the tomb of Heinrich II, which stands in the centre of the nave. This is the work of Tilman Riemenschneider who worked on it for some fourteen years, presumably on and off. The light was good and I was able to get some worth while shots of this and also of the old town hall. The building stands alone on an island; it was remodelled in the eighteenth century, and the façades are covered with quite startling 'trompe l'œil' frescoes. It is an unusual place with the rushing waters of the Regnitz all around.

After lunch I took the car and motored towards Coburg, part of the way following along the east bank of the river Itz on which that town stands. Coburg is almost cut off in a little torn-out peninsular of Western Germany that sticks into the under belly of East Germany. As I drove along, the atmosphere changed as though some strange theatrical impresario was working the switches. I found I was overtaken with a depressive foreboding feeling of something not quite right. The light appeared to go out of the countryside; the farms and villages became less cheerful.

The town I was approaching had plenty of history linked to it. Prince Albert, Consort of Queen Victoria, had been born there in 1819. The Saxe-Coburgs who had lived there from the sixteenth century onwards had made their way into a fair number of the Courts of Europe and by the seventeenth century you would have found them related to the Belgian, Bulgarian, English and Portuguese royal families. The town is dominated by one of the largest toughest looking fortresses in Germany, which has a double ring of fortified walls. The original castle dates from the twelfth century; but what one sees today is sixteenth century, and was built in the time of Johann Casimir. It was here that Luther lived during the Diet of Augsburg in

1530. There could have been a lot of things for me to see but this wasn't a visiting day.

Coburg clutters itself round the east side of the cold craggy pile which is crowned with the fortress, the Veste. The rocks are grey, the Veste is grey, and looking down on the town there is no change. The place creeps; behind each black tree-trunk on the hill leading up to the Veste lurks? You guess. CIA, West German agents, KGB, East German lads? It prickles with suspicion, intrigue. Looking down, if there is a following wind, one feels it would be possible to spit over the Fence, the Wall, for this macabre invention against communication wriggles its obscene way up and down the Bavarian landscape like some latter-day Australian rabbit fence. Wire, mines, watch-towers, the lot. 'I suppose my contact for this evening knows what he is doing,' I thought. 'I can think of more congenial places to meet. As for transporting the goods through that lot, I suppose a weasel might make it at odds of a hundred to one unless of course he has an arrangement.'

The hotel where we were to meet at eight o'clock was the Festungshof. I noted it as I quartered the town, taking my whereabouts. Later that evening at about half past six I parked the car in front of the hotel. I went in, found the bar, and had a couple of drinks, and went into the restaurant. I was not in a highly selective mood and just had one of those German confections of sausages, which despite their looks are surprisingly good.

By eight o'clock somebody – was it human? – came up to my table and paused.

The first impression had been inaccurate; it was human. About five feet two and square rather than round. I noticed the odour, a combination of damp onions, rabbits and Tabac after-shave. The clothes were obviously 'do-it-yourself' variety and hung suspended from various portions of the anatomy rather than fitting. A hand came out of a pocket, with the shortest fingers I've ever seen, all nearly the same length, the nails squared off with geometric precision. I glanced up at the face, which repeated this format. The eyebrows were a continuous straight line, even the corners of the eyes were square. The mouth an unpleasant crimson line, the jowls heavy with badly shorn black bristles.

"I – errr – sssssit" said a voice with an unfortunate sibilance. Somehow what looked like a solid block managed to bend roughly in the middle, and he sank into a chair opposite me.

"For me you wait?" was the query.

This linking up with a contact arranged for me by someone else scared the Y-fronts off me. I gave him a straight ten seconds burst eye-ball to eye-ball, and nothing happened. One mark to him. He interjected, "You haf finish." Neutral score with that one. He tried again: "I am thirrrrsday."

He must be getting as worried about this meeting as I was. I knew the correct phrase that would clinch matters; presumably he did as well. Unfortunately my Alsace friend in the hurry of packing me off had given me everything but some sort of description of what my contact would look like. But perhaps he had told him what I looked like because at last his face was starting to break up into what I imagined would eventually be a square smile if it ran to form. Watching the formative process was fascinating, the features were moving around as though a miniature earthquake was attacking the lower stratas of his facial anatomy. At last it was finished and almost with a click-stop the required degree of joy had been reached. With a burst of excitement he came out with the agreed phrase to which I replied with my half. We joined in some sort of strange temporary union.

"Drink?" I asked.

"Ja, Asbach und Pils," he came back with.

Well everyone to his taste. I fingered a waiter over, who sullenly approached. "One large Asbach and Pils and a large Dornats and Löwenbraü."

He offered me a cigarette, but I declined and took out a packet of cigars. He produced a lighter which exploded into a six-inch flame and we lit up. The drinks came and when I had paid, I lifted the Schnapps, "Prosit."

He replied in kind, and then came a rather jarring incident. A spider had been crawling up the wall beside the table, suddenly it dropped back on to the table and started to walk across in the direction of the ash-tray. I have seen people kill insects in quite a normal way. But the character I had just met squashed the innocent spider with a display of such violent unbridled brutality that a chill warning went through me. He raised his eyes from the pulverizing of the tiny body and went on, "We must walk in the woods; I will show you how the trees are planted. In Bavaria we like the trees."

Hells bells! This was going to be a jolly session. I knew years ago the Bavarians were crackpots for their forests. We finished our drinks in silence, and then he rose, "Now we will walk."

I followed him to the door and when we were out in the car park he turned to me and said, "We will go in your car. You drive. I direct."

I was quite relieved when I noticed that this two-legged tank didn't take me in the direction of Neustadt bei Coburg, which would have pitched us right up alongside the wire. Instead he chose a road that led towards Kronach. This ran along beside a very heavy dark pine forest, which clambered up the hills to the right. When we were about half-way between Coburg and Kronach he told me to slow down and look for a small turning on the right-hand side. This appeared as I was in the middle of a wide bend. He told me to turn in and drive up a little way. As I made the turn, my lights picked up the outlines of a grey van parked about fifty yards up in the woods. He told me almost at once to put my head-lights out. By the glimmer from the side-lights I drew up, following his instructions, alongside the van.

I was beginning bitterly to regret having been talked into this business by my Alsace acquaintance, and felt that it was not part of the pattern for the life that I had been following. This feeling was multiplied by two when the doors of the grey van opened and two near replicas of the chap beside me emerged. All three of them obviously used the same barber. My guide told me to put out the side-lights and get out with my package and to get into the back of the van which had now been opened up by the others. I couldn't quite make out what breed of vehicle it was, but it appeared to be one that was manufactured the other side of the wire. Nor could I make much sense of the number plate.

When the van doors were shut with the four of us inside the interior light was put on and it made rather a grim picture. The three sitting in a row on a bench set on one side; my guide holding a package which was presumably their contribution; me sitting on a similar seat the other side clutching my package. He signalled to me to exchange packages. We did. I undid. He undid.

Then began the most incongruous examination of paintings I've yet participated in, or shall I say the most weird place and conditions I have worked in.

He had his bundle of photographs and notes: I had my bundle of photographs and notes. We went to work. There was much whispering, hissing and chittering going on between the three opposite me. After about what seemed like an hour but I suppose was only about ten minutes, I found that his side of the bargain was in order, and I looked up to see the three of them beaming in some sort of unison. This I took to signify that my part of the bargain was in order with them.

I wrapped up the pictures they had given me. They wrapped up those I had given them. Then one of the characters who had been waiting in the van produced a flask and four glasses which he filled up, and we solemnly toasted each other. It was a slight surprise as I swallowed and found that it was good vodka.

My guide clapped me on my shoulder, opened the back doors of the van, said, "Auf Wiedersehen". I stepped down with the package, shook all three hands and turning round got into my car.

I started her up. Put on the side-lights, pulled the wheel round and was back on to the road in double, double time. I turned to the right at the bottom heading for Kronach. I didn't want to go back through Coburg. In Kronach I turned again to the right and returned to Bamberg by Lichtenfels. When I arrived I locked the car away and as I went up to my room I asked the porter if he would bring me a bottle of Asbach. With this I proceeded to calm down my yelping nerves for the night.

The next morning I was off good and early, and for some unknown reason I decided to go back a trifle indirectly. So took the road first of all to Schweinfurt before dropping down towards Würzburg and continuing south to Bad Mergentheim. Here I stopped for a lunch which I felt I had earned in the restaurant of the Viktoria. By three-thirty I was back on the E12 and by quite late that evening I delivered the goods to Alsace and collected in his usual currency.

*　　*　　*

There is no doubt that the art field is pulling money like no other magnet. I don't think anyone twenty-five years ago could have predicted the rise in prices for works of art. I know I felt there was a bonanza coming; but like the rest of them I never dreamt it was going to turn into a gusher. Studying periodicals and newspapers, looking at experts' opinions, brings out the facts. Since then the acceleration of figures in the sale-rooms has gone on by large multiples: Old Masters by between six and eight times; British pictures between nine and ten; Impressionists somewhere between sixteen and twenty; Old Master drawings twenty to twenty-five times; and then, somewhat surprisingly right at the top of the league, Old Master prints with a multiple ahead of thirty. Really one doesn't need to go in any further than this to realize why works of art continue to draw more and more the attentions of us, the likes of myself. But it is not only we who are hooked.

Turning back through various papers, I had come across an advertisement in February of this year (1975). Here an investor states he has got a large sum available and wants to acquire quality businesses in: art, galleries, antique furniture, jewellery, objets d'art, coin dealers, antiquarian booksellers, silversmiths, goldsmiths.

One sees announcements of art investment brokers breaking away from the confines of the city of London and setting up in the provinces. Their literature, of which I have copies, makes a strong point that the whole scheme they are offering is designed to provide maximum capital appreciation and investment and act as a hedge against inflation. One of the managing directors called the plan a form of capital usage most likely to provide aesthetic well-being, sound security and a very real opportunity for appreciation at rates in excess of the constant inflationary spiral which was now dogging most forms of investment!

All this explains why the word collector seems to be dissolving and becoming investor. In the last few years there have sprung into being the banker-backed establishments such as Artemis in Luxembourg which is apparently squirreling away the top cream of the painting market. This has caused me a lot of deep thought, for I have begun to realize that should I wish to continue my calling, I must really bring myself right up to date. It won't be easy to get hold of pictures that are stowed away thus and it will need some adjustment to means of approach and to techniques used. There is, however, a certain titillation and thrill from the idea of what might be rather hazardous exploits, which in certain moods I can find irresistible. Also I don't like the idea of pictures languishing in vaults doomed to be starved of the appreciation that should be theirs. Mr Hood has more than a strand of feeling for the painters who painted them.

Anyway I know where most of these premises are and have spent many a contented hour working out solutions with tactical exercises. Street plans, traffic flow, one-way streets, emergency services, road menders, power lines, water mains, gas mains, break-down gangs; these could be the pawns. Indeed, thinking back to some other ploys I have worked out, I can see no valid reason why this one should prove impregnable. Many eyebrows would be raised if their owners knew just what places I have been into. Secretive entry may be all right at times, but I have noted that for the big one there is nothing to beat assured refined bravado. I have used this simple formula many times. It is one of the most disarming tricks against a receptionist, a guard or a commissionaire.

*   *   *

I was over in England again at the end of July 1974 for yet

another go with some of the information Rina had given me. The first house had provided me with three fine horse paintings, and these had been followed up with a visit to a house near the Scottish border for the plucking of four good landscapes. I returned with them by sundry routes to my home. I was a little perplexed as to what I could do with the horse paintings since the departure of Robert. The decision in the end was that I would try Alsace yet again. I packed them up and motored to him.

This time as well I was met with a good deal of cordiality and enthusiasm. The landscapes were good and were by first-class international names, and so were the horses. These he was pleased with, I knew; yet I felt there was something else brewing, when suddenly he turned to me and said,

"My friend, there is a new market I've discovered, or rather it has found me. Can we get hold of some more of these pictures?"

"Well, yes I think I could," I replied. I thought of a prolific collector near Cologne who had such wares. I felt I could ask Alsace what was this new demand.

"Quite simply, it is the ones who are making all the money. I have been approached by a sheikh who wants just the type of paintings that you have walked in here with."

I thought to myself I'm not really very happy about getting mixed up in another of the Alsace schemes; although, to be sure, the other one two years ago, after the slightly hair-raising patch, had paid well enough.

Still, I discussed ways, means and figures with my friend, and the end of all this was that the plan was certainly going to show a very good profit. He told me the figures he would be asking the sheikh for these and others. This he divided into three, two parts for me, one for him. I must have held back a bit because he turned to me and went on,

"You know you needn't feel anxious, for don't forget, as I said before, you know who I am and where I live with the telephone number; but, as far as you are concerned, I don't know where you live; I don't even know if the name you have given me is a real one."

By the middle of August I returned to him with a further six horse paintings and eight more landscapes; not all British artists this time, but Dutch from the peak of the landscape school there, and one French. He looked over these twenty odd paintings and together we worked out a final figure. He put down his pen and said, "Now you leave these here. I shall start making the arrangements. Give me a call on the number you know in three or four days' time and I shall tell you what is to be done."

I rang him on the fourth day. He said that I must come and collect the paintings as soon as I could and that then he would give me the rest of the instructions.

When I got to him he told me that on a certain date in September I must take them to Langeais. If he remembered right, he said, this was a small town that was on the road that was north of the Loire, going westwards from Tours, and I should come to it just after Cinq Mars-la-Pile. He told me the time of day that I must be there. I was to park my car in the park at the back of the Château. At the time he had told me I should find waiting there a large Yugoslav Putnik coach, a cream and blue Setra. One person only would be in the coach. I must go over and say —— again he gave me a recognition phrase.

*   *   *

The day before the meeting was due I drove off towards Langeais, spending the night on the way. In the late evening of the next day I slowly approached the small town, as Alsace had suggested, via the road from Tours. I came into

Langeais and was confronted with the front of the Château, which has the appearance of a powerful medieval fortress. Immediately in front of the entrance I turned to the right passing the Café Rabelais with its painted red-brick and half-timbering, then left again at once into the narrow road that led to the car park.

I breathed a sigh of relief as I drew into the park, for there was the coach. The Yugoslav connection had worked.

I waited until exactly the time I had been given and then, making sure the park was deserted, I went across to the Setra. I gave a knock on the door. It was opened by a sallow-skinned, dark-haired man in an obviously unaccustomed European suit. We exchanged the necessary words and then exchanged packages.

The one I gave him was rather bulky, naturally with twenty-one paintings in it. The one he gave me was a soft leather wallet, but for a wallet it was also very bulky.

How he was going to repack the paintings I didn't know. I had ideas. I thought though he is going to have a busy hour or two fitting them into the places you can fit pictures which are not too large in coaches like that Setra, but where, of course, they mustn't show.

The following day I drove across for what was possibly the last call on Alsace. We divided the contents of the soft leather wallet.

I couldn't resist putting a few questions to him. How exactly did the sheikh work out that he was going to get the paintings?

He looked at me quite solemnly and said, "Maybe that is not something I should tell you."

But I pressed him because it was an interesting detail.

At last he went on, "It is not difficult. The Putnik coaches are becoming well known for tourist parties in Europe, even across to England. The coach has no trouble on the customs frontiers. It will go back to Yugoslavia with no difficulty. Then it will be unloaded, and I should think a car will take the paintings down to one of those little places on the coast near Split in the south. Here they will wait till one of those big fast motor launches can come across from Beirut. It's as easy as that."

*   *   *

The autumn of 1974 was pleasant and during the last few days of September I had sat peacefully at home. I had wandered out into the orchard and picked a basket or two of fruit. I had stood back and looked at the house and gardens. Slowly I began to realize an odd feeling of satiation was creeping up through me. I have had a good run. I have enjoyed it. After all it had been a well-planned exercise. There was more than enough banked away.

I went back into the house and for a time I was in my study musing round along the shelves; pulling out the odd drawer of a filing cabinet; leafing through a folio. Then I went across the hall into my drawing-room and poured out a long one, sat down and thought to myself, 'I think now retire, or shall I say I think I'll retire.' But I wouldn't be a hundred per cent certain that the taste won't come back.